Dealing
WITH
Difficult
People
IN THE
Library

Mark R. Willis

American Library Association
Chicago and London
1999

Text design by Dianne M. Rooney

Composition by D&G Limited in Minion and Frutiger using QuarkXpress 3.32

Printed on 50-pound white offset, a pH-neutral stock, and bound in 10-point coated cover stock by McNaughton & Gunn

The paper used in this publication meets the minimum requirements of American National Standard for Information Sciences—Permanence of Paper for Printed Library Materials, ANSI Z39.48-1992. ∞

Library of Congress Cataloging-in-Publication Data
Willis, Mark R.
    Dealing with difficult people in the library / Mark R. Willis.
       p.   cm.
    Includes bibliographical references and index.
    ISBN 0-8389-0760-1
    1. Libraries and readers—United States.   2. Communication in library science—United States.   3. Public libraries—Security measures—United States.   4. Public libraries—Public relations—United States.   I. Title.
    Z711.W64   1999
    025.5—dc21   99-20426

Printed in the United States of America.

03 02 01 00 99   5 4 3 2 1

This book is dedicated to my parents,
Robert and Clara Schupp,
who taught me to deal with difficult people
by using patience, compassion,
firmness, and humor.
Mom and Dad,
sorry I gave you
so many chances to practice.

Contents

SECTION II
Talking about Communication

SECTION III
Preventing Problems

APPENDIXES

Preface

Wait, don't skip this! I usually skip the prefaces to books too, but this preface will help you understand how the book works.

This book is for you, the person who works with library patrons every day. It is designed to be practical, giving ideas and examples that apply to the real library world. Philosophy and theory are great for late night chats, but workable solutions are what we need in the library world, and that's what this book is about. The suggestions are as specific as possible, developed to help you conquer those tough patron issues that make life at your library unpleasant. I think we can reduce significantly the number of difficult situations we encounter, so there are also suggestions on preventing problems.

I want to let you know just a little about me so you can understand where the approach for the book comes from. I'll make it brief.

For more than a decade, I have been the Community Relations Manager at the Dayton (Ohio) and Montgomery County Public Library. My duties include handling patron complaints and helping with difficult situations. Those of us in the library field understand that these difficult situations come up much more often than people expect. They can be anything from irritating to absolutely dangerous.

Like many library roles, this was something that came with the job, without any real training or preparation. I quickly began to feel comfortable with handling the toughest situations. It turns out my past and current experiences prepared me in ways I hadn't anticipated. My degree is in communication, and I saw that the education wasn't as useless as we had thought in college. (The old joke was, that on graduation day, communication majors received their diplomas and the keys to the cab they would be driving the next forty years.) However, those lessons from all those classes actually worked in the real world. If I had only known at the time, I might have paid more attention.

Before working at the library, I had jobs at the Easter Seal Society, a large law firm, the county government, and a few stints with retail. The Easter Seal job taught me how to work with people with all types of mental and physical disabilities, as well as their families and the bureaucrats who made their care decisions. It taught me to see stress in a whole new light.

At the Easter Seal Society, I worked with a mother in her forties taking care of her severely disabled teenager and trying to figure out how she could care for her child, who is getting bigger and sicker as the mother is getting physically weaker. That's true stress. The law firm taught me about dealing with demanding people—lawyers. As a paralegal who spent about half my time working with immigrants, I received an introduction to various cultures and how they deal differently with situations. Retail gave me experience with minor conflicts, especially checking IDs for alcohol (although many of my customers were members of a motorcycle gang, so I was never sure how minor any conflict was). As for the county government job, it simply taught me never to work for the county government again.

At the same time I started at the library, I embarked on a new experience that has become more important than I ever expected and has made a huge difference in my understanding of how to work with people. I volunteered for the Suicide Prevention Center (SPC) of Dayton to answer crisis telephone calls. I don't know what I thought would happen, but the result has been nothing short of life altering. The training was excellent, especially in listening skills and crisis communication. The actual calls, however, taught me more. When I came to the library and had to deal with someone unhappy over a missing book, I didn't get rattled because I had spent two hours on the phone the night before with someone holding a gun to his head. It was hard to feel stressed out by this patron after a call like that. The work with SPC taught me how to listen to people—not just their words, but the thoughts and feelings behind those words. It has helped me to learn how to connect with a person and work as a partner to solve whatever problem we're facing. It has also taught me the difference between a bad day and a catastrophe. Too many people think every minor bump on the road is a catastrophe when it's really just a day where things didn't go quite right. Understanding the difference has helped me more than I can explain.

That's more than enough about me. You should know that many of the ideas found here are not mine; they are from other people, other libraries, and even other fields. I have given talks on this topic at a number of library gatherings, and every time I walk away with several good suggestions that come from the audience during our discussions. I wish I could attribute every idea to the person I heard it from, but my memory isn't that good. The important fact is that many of my coworkers, both in the Dayton library and in libraries across the country, have contributed to this book. I hope the information is useful.

Thank you, and keep up the great work!

1

What's the Problem Here?

This book is designed to help the frontline staff of a public library prevent problems with patrons and to learn how to more effectively deal with problems when they do occur. I can hear nonlibrary folks now saying, "Problems? What kind of problems could those library workers have? They just sit around and read most of the time." If only the library world was as peaceful as outsiders envisioned it; we could all be reading Hemingway instead of this book.

The reality of library work is different. No facility in the nation hosts a more diverse collection of people on a daily basis. We have entrepreneurs, preschoolers, college students, senior citizens, attorneys, and homeless people: all races, ages, and social standings. The reasons people flock to libraries are equally varied. They come to learn to read, finish a doctoral dissertation, write a business plan, find out what kind of puppy they should get, check out audiovisual items, attend programs, use the computers, and more. There are also nonlibrary reasons—to get out of the weather, meet friends after school, break up a lonely afternoon, enjoy free day care, and even act out their criminal motivations, such as finding a purse to steal or more possibilities we don't even want to think about.

Every day, this mix of people with their variety of purposes wanders into our buildings, some for a couple of minutes, others for all day and night. Essentially, we are running a big day-care center where we need to get this diverse group of people to follow rules, sit quietly, and play nicely with each other. We can't even bribe them with milk and cookies.

How do we accomplish this task? Are we like a lion tamer without a whip and a chair? Maybe, but that's not so bad. A lion tamer succeeds because of his ability to stay calm, focus on his task, and *work* with his lions, not *against* them. That's how we can manage our wildest situations and the mix of people we serve. We don't need the whip and chair (good thing too—our business manager might approve the chair, but the whip could be a problem). Let's catalog some of the challenges we face in dealing with difficult patrons.

Staff dealing with unfamiliar situations

Whether you have an M.L.S. from a prestigious university or a high school degree from someplace average, nobody comes to a library job trained and prepared to face all the odd situations we can encounter. Talking a drunk out of the building may be part of our job, but it's seldom part of our training. Even if we are trained on some aspects of the people issues, we never know when a new situation may pop up. For example, a children's librarian may be the best in the world at getting the little people to peacefully enjoy the library, but this same librarian might not be prepared for dealing with the child's grandmother, who starts yelling about a controversial book in the children's room. Even if we specialize, there's no guarantee that our patrons will abide by our choices. We have to be ready to take on the entire range of human problems.

Lack of library training for tough patron issues

When your library first started using computers, most likely there was some kind of staff training and a bit of practice time when starting up. Libraries often do not give nearly as much training on tough patron issues as staff want or need. The library board will be sure it has a computer savvy staff, but that staff is often more concerned about what to do when a mom knocks her kid down. The "people training" is usually less frequent and intense than the technical skills programs.

Time to deal with a difficult customer

Most library staff stay busy handling the routine duties, which means there isn't spare time to concentrate on that one person who wants to complain endlessly about something you can't change anyway. The trouble is that some of these people will get more upset if they feel ignored, and then no one can overlook them. If we had taken the time to begin with, we could have avoided the problem completely, but we don't always have the luxury of focusing on one person for an extended period of time.

An administration that doesn't quite get it

Give the administration the benefit of the doubt—they mean well. But, especially in larger libraries, the top management does not spend much time with the customers, and they really don't know the day-to-day issues. They may only have direct patron interaction when they are listening to a complaint about how you mistreated someone, while not hearing the fact that this person first called you every name in the book. They talk about security, staff training, wanting input from everybody, and so forth, but their actions fail to convince staff that they are serious. When you are the one stuck dealing with all the tough situations, well-meaning bosses are not enough.

Budgets that limit security options

In most communities, money for libraries is becoming harder to find. When there is a little extra, it goes into new computers, overdue building repair, or shoring up the material collection. Adequate money for quality security guards and other preventive measures is scarce. It's not that the need is overlooked; it's just hard to find the resources to meet the need.

First Amendment issues

In our world, we think of the First Amendment as protecting our right to free speech. There's a little more to it than that. It also includes the right of free assembly. That means that most people have a right to be in your library. We still have the authority to throw a person out of the library with adequate cause, but the First Amendment says that this removal is a big deal. It has to be done following certain, often unclear, criteria and is subject to legal action. Libraries can be intimidated into allowing all sorts of people to remain in the building out of fear of legal repercussions.

Public pressure

Is it harder to argue with a patron around tax levy time? Lots of staff would say yes. The homeless guy may not get any special treatment, but the mom who ignores her screaming kids might not get the same response from the staff a week before a levy vote as the week after. We are also aware of friends of our commissioners and trustees, because they make themselves known to us. We want to be fair and treat everyone the same, but nobody wants to be the one who offends a commissioner. Libraries need money and that means it's risky to offend those who control the money, regardless of whether it's the voters or members of our funding body (and their families, friends, dentists, etc.).

Peer pressure—it's not just for teenagers anymore

If you work at a circulation desk where other staff clearly pride themselves on collecting every penny of overdue fines, it will be hard for you to write off the occasional fine when common sense dictates.

When we think of "corporate culture," we think of banks and their stuffy traditional dress codes or Silicon Valley computer companies where programmers wear T-shirts and work twenty-two hours a day. However, libraries have a corporate culture too. There are some general similarities among libraries, but much of the culture is determined by your coworkers, especially those with seniority. This culture thrives more on the personal than the professional, on politics rather than policy. This begins to sound ominous but can work for us as well as against us. If we insist on great customer service, new employees will pick up on this. We can create a culture where peer pressure quietly encourages great customer service.

Our constantly changing environment

For decades the library was the symbol of stability. Nothing changed inside these silent rooms. Now change is our motto, and every week seems to bring something new. We are inundated with new computers, new services, new programs, new customers, new complaints, new laws, new material, plus new confusion for staff and customers. As soon as we get close to learning all the answers, the world changes the questions. We're running uphill on ice wearing slippery shoes, and the world thinks we sit around and read.

Library work is diverse and so are the challenges we face in doing our work, especially on the people front. Fortunately, there are ways to meet every challenge.

Workable Solutions—an Overview

So we have to accept that we have a uniquely diverse clientele wanting to do all sorts of things in an understaffed building. We can handle this. A simple plan of action can effectively improve our dealings with patrons:

Goals

1. Develop communication skills to handle even the toughest situation.
2. Create policies that reduce problems.
3. Train all library staff in any area that affects their dealings with patrons.

Guidelines

Develop Communication Skills

The first step is to learn to successfully handle the problems we know we will face. More than anything else, we need to use good communication skills. This means

> listening effectively to understand the issues presented by the customer
>
> keeping an open mind to understand all points of view, whether we agree or not
>
> speaking in a manner that shows we understand and care
>
> giving a clear response that the customer can easily comprehend

Once we get our communication skills down, these difficult situations will be less trying. There's a real pleasure in turning around a potentially unpleasant situation. When a patron is on the verge of blowing his top and you are the one who can work with him to keep everyone under control, you have an accomplishment of real value.

Anyone who wants to can learn to handle these situations. One of the barriers to better communication is the widely held belief that communicators are born, not made. That's false. Maybe we can never learn to give inspiring oration like Jesse Jackson, but fortunately we don't need to. Our communication needs are skills that can be learned. There are specific techniques that can improve anyone's ability to understand the person he or she is conversing with and to respond in an effective manner. These techniques are no more difficult to learn than any other skills we have had to acquire to do our jobs. It's a matter of making an effort to improve and then learning and practicing the same way we acquire any other skills.

Create Policies That Reduce Problems

In addition to handling problems, look for ways we can prevent as many problems as possible. Closing the library doesn't count, although it is a way to reduce problems. There are less drastic methods to reduce our difficult situations. As boring as it sounds, good policies are a solid starting point. Nothing fancy or dramatic is required, just common sense clearly stated. There are plenty of places to start, which should make our life a little easier.

The policies, like our nation's laws, are only as good as their application and enforcement. That means all the library staff need to be trained on what the policies are, how to enforce them, and what to do when something goes wrong. With this information and training, staff will discover that most situations will be a matter of following policy in the way they have been taught. We shouldn't have to deal with very many unexpected circumstances. We know what common problems we face, and we can plan for them.

Train All Library Staff

Training for staff is crucial. Training can prepare a staff member to handle most situations. Knowing what your options are before you dive in will prevent you from getting in over your head.

Summary

Improved communication skills, policies, and training won't solve all your library problems. They will help, however, if you make a commitment to learning new skills and using those skills. There are times when the effort may not seem worthwhile, but in the long run the results will justify your work. Your library will run smoother, and your life will be more pleasant. That should be worth a little effort anyway.

2

Gaining Control

If you can keep your head about you when everyone else is losing theirs, you probably don't understand the situation.

—Anonymous

It starts off simply enough, like many average transactions.

A customer comes in and says he received a notice that we are holding a book on reserve for him. After some checking, we can't locate the book, and suddenly this patron starts yelling about the importance of this book and how we are messing up his life by losing this vital book.

Another time you're shelving books, and a well-dressed man asks if you can help him for a moment. The next thing you know, he's asking you about the sex books and if you want to look through them with him.

You see someone eating at one of the study tables, food wrappers strewn all over. You politely mention the "no eating" policy, and all of a sudden the diner is tossing the wrappers on the floor and yelling, "No one tells me where I can't eat!"

We never know when we will face a potential confrontation. It can spring from a typical activity like checking out a book or from the more unusual. Either way, we are now expected to handle the situation and deal with all the unknowns it brings.

Any customer conflict can leave us struggling for control because we misdirect our struggle. On control, we need to realize three things:

1. We *can* control ourselves.

2. We *can* control the situation.

3. We *cannot* control other people.

Our failures often come when we overlook the first two and focus on the third, which is a doomed effort (unless you have a Taser or other police equipment not on the supply lists of most libraries).

But let's talk first about self-control. There are some steps we can take to help us achieve and maintain self-control. Chapter 3 covers controlling the situation; and, in a very big way, the rest of this book is devoted to helping readers understand and deal with the fact that, although we cannot control other people, we can manage the situation to a successful resolution for all concerned.

Controlling Ourselves

Let's start with the easy one—controlling ourselves. That seems like a simple enough proposition, especially at the library. We are usually comfortable in our friendly library work environment. We know our coworkers, which ones are experts in certain areas, whom we can count on to help us, and whom we can count on to call in sick around a long weekend. We know the collection, the policies, where the break room is, and how many days until payday. This is our library and things are pretty much under control.

Maybe that's why a difficult patron can do such a good job at rearranging our world, or at least our day. In this comfortable, controlled environment we now have a wild card not following our carefully designed plans for the day.

Our first step in gaining control of the situation is getting control of ourselves. You are in charge of the situation and can only control it if you control yourself. If we fail to control ourselves, we can't expect to have any success in dealing with a challenging situation. Fortunately, there are some tried and true techniques to help us.

Pause and take a deep breath

This is one of the oldest pieces of advice around, but there is a reason that it's still around. It works. Everyone from singers and athletes to yoga practitioners will tell you about the benefits of proper breathing. One good, slow breath is a proven way to start gathering your internal resources and preparing to handle the situation. Anytime things look like they will get tough, make this your first action.

Never take it personally

Today, Joan overslept, got yelled at by her boss for being late, broke the heel of her favorite shoe, had an argument with a friend, and couldn't find a parking place before stopping in the library. You get to tell her that the copy of *It's a Wonderful Life* she stopped in for can't be found anywhere. Congratulations! You win today's "Bad Timing Award" for being in the wrong place at the wrong time.

It's important to remember when someone is jumping all over you that it's not you she is really upset with. It may be the situation, the person herself, the library's policy, or life in general, but it's not you. That's not easy to keep in mind when someone is going on about "the incompetents at this library," but it's the truth. Say to yourself, "This isn't about me, this isn't about me. . . . " Realizing this will help us keep our self-control.

Understand your own hot-button issues

Everyone has issues he or she is sensitive about. I have a coworker who grew up in a household where there was some loud arguing, which caused family tension. Now she is very uncomfortable when a patron starts to get loud. On the other hand, she is great with our off-the-wall patrons, people other staff hide from. If a patron she is working with gets loud, I immediately try to step in because I know she is extremely uncomfortable in these circumstances. On the other hand, she will happily help with other people's "reality-challenged" customers.

The first step is to recognize what pushes our buttons. Then we should see if we can get someone who doesn't share our same sensitivity to assist with a patron who pushes those buttons. The more demanding or upset that patron is, the more important it is that we try to get assistance.

Keep your sense of humor

If you don't have one, *get one* because there are few attributes more important in any kind of public service than a sense of humor. That includes the ability to laugh at ourselves. If you can keep a smile on the inside, it is unlikely you will lose your self-control. Remember, he who laughs, lasts.

Here's a case study:

> In a discussion of patron problems we encounter at the library, one library staff member told a story about a frequent library user who had an idea he felt strongly about. He made repeated suggestions to staff and to administration, and he even went to board meetings to press his case. Unfortunately, it simply wasn't workable, and he refused to accept that fact. To get a measure of satisfaction, he drafted his young children to help. Whenever he would bring them into the library, he would ask the kids, "Where are we now?" and they would answer as he trained them: "We're in the bad library, Daddy." This, of course, annoyed the staff, which was exactly his goal. What would you do?
>
> After talking about it for awhile, it was agreed that there really wasn't anything to do but laugh about it. Any type of argument with Daddy would be just what he wanted. The best approach is to laugh and realize that if that's the worst thing that happens all day, you've had a pretty good day.

Rudeness happens

Accept that we do have to tolerate some rudeness (but we don't have to tolerate abuse!). Joe comes in three minutes before closing and has to have two books and a magazine article about capital punishment for his child's book report. You interrupt your closing procedures, dig up two books and quickly locate an article, get change to copy the magazine article, and finish everything in less than five minutes, which means you don't get out until late, but it's worth it because you provided quality service. Joe rains on your parade as he walks out grumbling, "I can't believe it took so long to get a few books."

Any public service work means sometimes encountering people who don't appreciate your efforts. They can be brusque, lack manners, and generally make you glad you aren't stuck in an elevator with them. It's a reality we have to accept in this line of work. Abusive treatment is something different, and no staff should have to tolerate that. We'll look at the distinction later. But for better or worse, that occasional case of rudeness comes with the job and we have to expect it. The best way to handle it is to see the preceding technique ("Keep your sense of humor").

A True Self-Control Story (nonlibrary)

In college, I used to play lots of table tennis and got fairly good. I had one friend who was better than me but never won. Here's why —as he would get within a few points of victory, I would throw the ball across the room, roll it under the table, leave it on my side of the table and refuse to get it for him, and basically find any way I could to annoy him. Unfortunately for him, this tactic always had the same result. He would get angry, lose control, and soon lose the game. He got mad and made stupid mistakes, mistakes he would never make when he kept calm. He never beat me, despite being a superior player.

For my friend, there is a happy ending to this story. He joined the U.S. Air Force and was accepted into training as a fighter pilot. In a solo training flight over the desert, his plane malfunctioned. He tried to overcome the mechanical difficulties but couldn't. At the last minute, he ejected to safety. In this life-or-death situation, he found the self-control he never could master during Ping-Pong, and it saved his life. I wouldn't have a chance of beating him today.

If we look at the importance of our daily dealings with patrons, most of them are more important than a friendly game of table tennis and less important than a crash at 600 mph. Regardless, maintaining self-control is the first step toward handling any difficult situation.

3

Controlling the Situation

You're dealing with a difficult patron issue. You've got yourself under control. Now, what can you do to get control of the situation and resolve it before it becomes worse?

Here are some basic steps:

Listen

Your listening skills may be your most valuable tool in any challenging situation. Really listening carefully to what is being said has several benefits. First, it gives you the information you need to formulate an intelligent response. Second, it makes the patron feel respected and connected. The last thing we want to do is make someone feel powerless. When that happens, we'll have the patron fighting to gain power, in addition to arguing over whatever the initial issue was. That can mean anything from yelling to uttering the phrase all librarians despise, "I'm a taxpayer, and I pay your salary!" That comment will do nothing to improve our service. Most of us usually think, "Then when do I get my raise?" That phrase, along with shouting and other unpleasant behaviors are all attempts by patrons to reach the same goal—to be heard. That's all. We can frequently prevent patrons from having to take such extreme approaches by listening carefully from the start and letting them know we are listening.

Always take a moment before responding. Too often we move to immediately start listing rules or giving the company line on policy before we have completely heard the person out. That causes several problems. In the first place, we don't get the information we need to respond properly. More important is the impact it has on the person and the situation. When we fail to hear him out, that's taken as a sign of disrespect. To the patron it can come across as treating him as less than a person.

Listening is worth an entire chapter, so we'll discuss it further in chapter 15.

Look at it from the patron's point of view

Susie is a nurse who works from 3 P.M. to 11 P.M. at a big hospital. She's worked this shift for years, and many of her friends and associates naturally are on that same schedule. She came into the library one Saturday and complained about the hours. "You should stay open until 1 A.M., at least. I'd love to come in after work and get a few books and videos. Lots of my friends tell me they would come in after work if you were open. There are factory workers, police officers, and lots of others who work the same hours we do. You'd get lots of business."

Now, to most of us, the idea of keeping the library open that late is silly. We know it's all we can do to afford to stay open the hours we currently have. We also worry about whom we could get to work those hours even if we did have the money. And what kind of clientele would wander into the library then? It's easy to quickly dismiss Susie's idea, but to her and the other people in her nocturnal world, this is as logical as keeping Denny's open all night.

Instead of dismissing her idea, offer to pass it on to the director, and ask Susie if she would like the director to contact her with a response. Although it's unlikely this idea will fly, at least we can show Susie the courtesy of listening to it.

Acknowledge the patron's feelings

These are human interactions we have at the desk. Despite well-crafted policies, automated systems, and laser checkouts, we still cannot take the human being out of the equation. If we have a patron who has gone out of her way to pick up a book that's listed as available only to discover it's missing, it may not be enough to offer to put a reserve on it or send her to another branch to get a copy there. It helps to say, "I realize this is inconvenient for you." In a case such as this, we can't make the book she wants magically appear, so maybe we can't meet this patron's library need at that moment.

We can recognize her feelings and treat the patron as a living, breathing person with feelings. Besides this being the right thing to do, it has the side benefit of encouraging the patron to treat us in the same manner.

It's okay to apologize, even if you did nothing wrong

We are often reluctant to apologize because it seems to imply that we did something wrong. If my friend's dog dies, it's natural to say, "I'm sorry your dog died." That, of course, does not mean I killed the dog. It simply demonstrates the fact that we recognize the other person's unhappy situation. In the case of Susie, it makes sense to say, "I'm sorry our hours aren't convenient for you" before talking to her about passing her suggestion to the director. We aren't blaming anyone, just showing that we understand things aren't right for her.

Monitor nonverbal cues, both your own and the patron's

You cannot *not* communicate. Even if you are silent, you are communicating. Ask anyone in sales. Salespeople will tell you that "you can't sell anything to a guy who has his arms crossed." Although that may be a bit of an exaggeration, these salespeople make a living reading others and know to pay careful attention to body language. Some studies say that more than half of what is communicated is not through your words but through your body language, facial expressions, and voice tone. So even if we work hard to choose our words carefully to avoid a blowup, we need to take equal care in how our body and tone of voice are communicating.

We also want to be aware of patrons' body language. Are they sending signs that they are rejecting our comments? Stepping back, looking away, fidgeting, and a confrontational facial expression all indicate we are not getting through, even if the patrons are silent. Maybe it's time to try a different approach or get someone else to talk with them. Watching is really part of listening and gives us more information about how our conversation is going.

Focus on the library issue at hand

Customers don't come to us with an agenda in hand. They can present any number of ideas at once, often intermingled. It's not unusual to hear a story that involves a library complaint blended with several personal issues. Things can get out of control if we lose focus on what we are trying to accomplish.

Sometimes that is more difficult than it sounds. What if patrons can't or don't want to focus on the library issue? Maybe they are upset, muddled, or unclear.

Here is an example of such an unclear issue:

> I have a question. My mother's sick and the stupid doctors can't make up their minds what to do. One day they tell us one thing, and another day it's completely different. And the insurance company is always disagreeing with the doctors about everything, and I don't know if they will pay for anything at this point. I was looking for several books, and they either aren't on the shelf or they don't tell me what I need to know. I was here yesterday, but the guy I talked to yesterday was worse than useless. He didn't help at all.

How do you respond? Does she want books about her mother's medical condition? Consumer information on dealing with insurance companies? Help finding a book listed as available? Maybe she wants to make a complaint about the "guy I talked to yesterday." She's given us about half a dozen issues and no indication on what she really wants. The only way to make any progress here is to get some clarification from the patron to help both you and her focus on the next step. We need to say, "What can I do to help you?" Let the patron take the first step to clarification. In a case like this one, where the patron feels she has had trouble here earlier, it may help to acknowledge those concerns. A simple statement such as, "I'm sorry you have had trouble finding what you're looking for," before going on to the specific information needs may help. This shows a recognition of her recent difficulties and may do a little to overcome any resistance she has. Remember, this is a human interaction and the more comfortable the patron is, the smoother it will go. Additionally, she may have a legitimate complaint that needs to be considered.

A good approach is to repeat back the request from the patron, clarifying and summarizing what you believe is the request. "You want some basic information about skin cancer and its treatment. Is that right?" *Then* take a moment and let the patron respond. Sometimes we are starting to look up books on the topic before the patron says, "No, I just want a good novel to read while she's in the hospital."

Although I don't believe we can control another person, treating him or her with respect at all times is as close as we can come. That way we can eliminate the patron's need to fight for power and respect and we can focus on the library issue. And that's much better than wrestling with someone's struggle for humanity.

A Nonlibrary Example

A friend of mine had severe headaches and was told by a doctor that the cause could be a brain tumor. Although the doctor advised her this was unlikely, he still wanted to get it checked and sent her to a hospital for a CAT scan. She arrived, nervous about the procedure, worried about the possible results, and still suffering from headaches. She was ushered into a small waiting room and was told she was next. The nurse was on her way out and told the technician, "I've got a head for you."

My friend, to her credit, said, "I'm an entire person." The nurse muttered an apology and left.

It's easy to see how the hospital staff can look at a person and see a disease or a test to be done. We can do the same thing at libraries, seeing an overdue fine or a lost reserve instead of a person. In the course of a single day, we may see lots of these situations. In the years we work at a library, the number climbs into the thousands or more. But to the patrons, theirs is a unique experience, and we need to remember their point of view. If we do, we will go a long way toward controlling the vast majority of situations.

4

Turning Complainers into Happy Customers

Sooner or later, we all have to deal with an unhappy patron. This isn't the person who says, "You should have more copies of *Police Academy 4*." This is the person who says, "I can't believe what goes on in this place! What a waste of tax dollars!"

These are patrons who have more than a simple information need; they also have an issue with staff or management of the library. They may have already encountered staff who have, in their minds, treated them rudely, ignored them, been incompetent, or all of the above. Or they may have a real disagreement with our policies, collection, or service.

We really have several challenges here. We have to deal with whatever made them complain in the first place (a missing book, bad service, etc.). We have to deal with the fact that they are upset, which means calming them down and avoiding a real conflict. Finally, we have to handle the fact that they want to lodge a complaint, formally or informally.

For this unhappy person, we need to use all of our interpersonal skills. The first few moments of an encounter with someone who is upset and complaining are pivotal. If we handle the situation correctly, the patron normally will calm down and we can proceed. If we don't, there is a good chance that the patron can become more upset, and we are faced with anything from an embarrassing incident to an actual dangerous situation.

Goals

1. Find out what the exact problem is.
2. Fix or respond to the problem.
3. Prevent the problem and the situation from getting worse.
4. See if this problem can be prevented in the future.

Guidelines

Here are some basic measures we can take to prevent bad situations.

Be sure you understand exactly what the problem is
This goes back to our listening skills. We have to take enough time and be sure we have an accurate perception of the real issue at hand, not assume we know. Sometimes this means asking follow-up questions to clarify the patron's concerns. When a person has a complaint, the last thing we want to do is misunderstand the issue and go off in the wrong direction. Even if we are well-intentioned, that will just get our patron more upset.

Get a supervisor to assist if this is an issue you are not authorized to handle
Let the patron know if you can't take care of this yourself. "That's the policy of our Board of Trustees, and I have to follow it. I can get a supervisor who might be able to help you." Even if it is something your supervisor cannot or will not change, it is important that the patron realizes you are doing all you can. When you are not doing what the patron wants you to do, it's important to prevent the "me against you" situation, which can lead to things becoming personal. The patron needs to understand that you are not the problem and that you are doing all you can to be of assistance.

If no supervisor is available, write down the problem so it can be passed on
It is amazing how writing down a complaint can do so much to satisfy a customer.

It makes the person feel respected and like you are doing all you can. It's almost as if you are on the patron's side and are working with her to get this horrendous library failing corrected. Get all of the details you can, and find out if the patron would like to be contacted. If so, be sure to get a phone number and ask when the best time to reach her is. Don't promise an unreasonably prompt reply. Your promise may make the patron happy at the moment, but things will be even worse if it's not kept. If you know the responsible person is out for a week, pass that information on, saying something such as, "The director personally handles requests such as this, but I know she's out for at least a week, so unfortunately it will be ten days or so before we can get a response to you. I'm sorry about the delay."

Ask the patron to write it down

Sometimes, a patron is so disjointed that it's impossible to figure out exactly what the issue is. Have him write down the information so it can be passed on. Provide paper (not a little slip but a nice-sized sheet or two —it will make the handwriting easier to read) and something to write with. This is also a good way to deal with someone when you have a line at the desk, a program starting, the phone ringing, and the computers just went down. You can't use "write it down" as a substitute for addressing a problem, but if you've been through the other steps and you are at a point where the patron wants something only the director, board, or someone who is unavailable can help with, it's a useful approach.

Be sure to find out if the patron wants any follow-up and, if so, that he or she has included a phone number or other contact information. I don't like to skip that step and assume we have the records in our files. The patron could have moved or may wish to be called at work or some other number we don't have.

Situation: Bad Example

Dan, a reasonably well-dressed, middle-aged man comes to the circulation desk with a reserve notice in his hand. He seems impatient, upset. Terrie, a two-year veteran of the circ desk, waits on him.

"May I help you?" she asks.

"You better be able to. I've been waiting for this book for more than a month; then, I got this notice last night. The notice says the book will be held only until the fifteenth, but I didn't even get the notice until the sixteenth. I don't know why you never send these notices out in time for someone to get his book," he says.

"Most people get them in time. What's your name?" she asks.

"Dan Jones," he says. "I never get my notices on time. This happens all the time to me. Last time I told them to call me instead of wasting postage, but apparently no one wants to save money."

"We don't have enough staff to call for every reserve. There's nothing on the reserve shelf for you, Mr. Jones."

"Not on the shelf?! Well, where is it?"

"It would have gone to the next person who requested it, I suppose."

"Look, I'm supposed to have that book, and I put it on reserve and waited. Now you people screw up and I'm without," he is now shouting. "It's your fault, and you need to call whoever has the book and get it for me!"

"I can't do that," Terrie says. "It's the post office's fault you didn't get your notice on time."

"Always blaming someone else. You know how long it takes to get the mail delivered. You should allow enough time. Either get me that book now, or I'm going straight over to city hall and talk to the mayor about the way this library wastes money and mistreats taxpayers!"

The line is growing, and everyone is staring at the two involved in this escalating exchange. Terrie is getting frustrated and angry. Her supervisor is not around, and the only other people at the desk are a trainee and a library aide.

"Look, I can't get the book for you. The only thing I can do is to put it on reserve again for you. I don't know when the book will become available."

"On reserve?!? I just tried that, and you couldn't get it for me that way! Why in the hell should I try that again?"

"Well, there's nothing else I can do for you. Next."

"You're not done with me! You can't wait on someone else, you idiot!!" Dan shouts, getting in the way of the next-in-line patron, who was timidly trying to move around him and get her books checked out.

We'll leave our happy couple here, both angry, frustrated, and generally unhappy with the world.

This may not be how most people respond to a missing reserve or some other minor snafu at the library, but anyone who works at the library long enough learns that there are a few who drastically overreact. These are the ones who can mean big problems—whether they make a big stink with our funders, create a scene at the library, become enraged to the point of being dangerous, or simply add big heaps of unwanted stress to our day. Learning how to control these situations is an important and learnable skill.

Making Customers Happy

So, to avoid the hassle Terrie ended up with, How do we proceed?

We need to remember our steps in the previous chapters about controlling ourselves and the situation. Start with a brief pause, take that deep breath, and face the patron in a calm state of mind. We need to remember not to take comments personally and to focus on the library issue as much as possible.

Identify the Problem

The first step is to find out what the problem is. This can start with a simple "Can I help you?" statement. When it's someone we have reason to believe is unhappy, expect that the first response may be sarcastic or rude. Don't let that sidetrack you, or you will end up in a pointless argument. In our example, Dan replies with a bit of a challenging comment, indicating that he is either in a bad mood or anticipating a problem.

Remember, *you don't have to respond to every comment.* Stick to the main issue. If you aren't sure what the issue is, then repeat the request as you understand it back to the patron. Although Dan is unhappy with the timing of the reserve notice and wonders about us calling instead of mailing, his main issue seems to be trying to get the book he wants.

Meet the Need

Terrie should check to see if there is any way to meet his book need. She could look for another copy in the system, try interlibrary loan, see if there is an older edition that might work, or suggest a similar book with the information he needs. Depending on your library, such actions may mean getting a reference librarian to help. If you need to shuffle an upset patron to another staff member, do this with utmost care. Over the years, I have found the most upset people we have to deal with started with a small problem and were shuffled around, often to the wrong places. They end up more angry about the shuffling than with whatever the initial problem was. In this case, if Terrie needs to refer Dan to another staff member, it's best if she walks with him to the proper place and explains the situation briefly. "Mr. Jones got his notice late about a book we had on reserve for him, and now it's out to someone else. We don't have another copy in the system. Could you check interlibrary loan for him or see if there is anything similar available? He really needs this information quickly."

In addition to possibly finding what he needs, the personal attention shows a good faith effort, which will reduce the likelihood that he will see Terrie as someone who doesn't care about his plight. When he sees Terrie as a partner in helping him solve this problem, it's much less likely he will get angry at her personally. If a patron is going to get angry, we want the anger to be directed at the situation or some vague system, not an individual.

Consider Policy Changes

What about his complaint about getting notices late before?

We have to consider that sometimes we need to change the way our library does things. If we have heard this complaint from time to time, maybe we aren't allowing adequate time for patrons to pick up their reserves. Maybe there are other methods of notification we should explore. One of the most dangerous phrases in the English language is, "We've always done it that way." Change is part of daily life for all of us and that includes the library. Any staff member who notices problems has the duty to bring them to the attention of library management. If the director doesn't work on the circulation desk, how will he or she know that we get several people every day who receive their notices late?

Alert Top Management

All staff have a duty to pass on information about concerns to management, and management have the responsibility to listen seriously to those comments. When reporting a problem to management, it's best to quantify the problem. How often do we have the problem? Has it been going on for a while or has it just been recognized? Is it worse at some times than others? The more information you can give, the easier it is to respond. It often helps to suggest a solution when reporting the problem. "In the last month, we have had two or three people come in every day and say they didn't get their notice until past the time allotted to pick up their reserve materials. It's making for some unhappy patrons and stressing out the staff who have to deal with it. Is it possible to change so the patrons have 10 days rather than one week to pick up their reserve?"

One way to judge an excellent organization is how quickly bad news reaches the top. In Dan's case, Terrie might have stayed with the reference librarian while he or she was looking for an interlibrary loan copy of the book. Terrie could bring up the problem with getting notices late. She could say to Dan, "You said you have had problems with notices getting to you late. I don't have the authority to change that system, but I can pass your concern on to the director if you like."

"Yes, I would. This has happened several times, and it gets annoying," Dan replies.

"I'll certainly tell Ms. Dewey, our director. Would you like her to give you a call about this?"

It's understandable that most of us don't like complaints. We have to face an unhappy patron plus the fact that our library may have messed up. No one wants to hear this. We like our libraries and think we are doing a pretty good job, especially with the overburdened staff and inadequate budgets we live with. The fact is, we have to hear complaints sometimes. Our immediate duty is to that individual patron with the problem. Then we need to consider if this complaint is pointing out a problem that affects others. If so, it's to the library's advantage to explore ways to reduce these complaints. We don't want to hear them, but complaints may alert us to needed change. In the long run, that's a positive for everyone.

5

Real Problem Cases

Now we're getting to the serious stuff, beyond the patron with a problem into the problem-patron territory. These are the ones who move past the *annoying* label and into the *scary* category. They can range from people on drugs to the mentally ill. We may see them angry, acting erratic, or exhibiting sexually harassing characteristics or signs of mental illness. Sometimes they are actual library patrons, and other times they just happen to be in our building.

Although problem patrons represent a small group, they are frightening and dangerous enough that every library needs to spend time preparing for such situations. First, let's try to weed out the *potential* problems from the *real* problems. Some people who seem to have the capability to create a major incident can be defused if we are careful and lucky in our initial contact with them. To begin with, we need to keep our previous lessons in mind. Just because someone is more serious than most of our patrons is no reason to abandon our interpersonal skills. This is when we need them the most. Treat the patron like a library patron first and a problem patron *only* when circumstances warrant.

1. Stay calm. Pause, take a deep breath, and focus. We can't control the situation unless we can control ourselves. The more frightening or

bizarre the patron, the tougher this task is, yet the more crucial it is, too. Remember that you can handle this, and if things get out of control, you will call the police and let them deal with it.

2. Listen to the patron. Even if the patron is confusing and may seem off the wall, careful listening may help us find out what is needed.

3. Focus on the library issue. Even the most confused person may have a library question or issue. If we can help with that, the patron will usually stay calm and move on with no difficulty.

One of our most famous patrons will come up to a reference desk or walk into an office and ask, "Is Dayton a big city?" The first time it happened to me, I tried the normal library responses, giving Dayton's population, rank compared to other cities, and so on. He responded to every answer with, "Is Dayton a big city?" Finally, a light came on in my thick head, and I said, "Yes, Dayton is a big city." He asked me about a few other nearby towns, and I gave him a yes-or-no answer. He thanked me and left happy. He still comes in every few months with the same questions, and I give him the same answers and he leaves happy. I could try to pigeonhole him into our standard way of doing things, but he would never fit. Once I learned that he wanted a yes-or-no answer, I could make him happy and finish the exchange in a minute or two, a small amount of time compared with the time I had to spend before this simple discovery.

For a few, this isn't enough. Not everyone will happily wander off with a yes-or-no answer. We have those who are screaming, hallucinating, arguing, harassing, or behaving in some way that suggests they may be a continuing, serious disruption and possibly dangerous. For these, we have to shift to serious mode. Our goals and guidelines should be as follows:

Goals

1. Stay calm and keep everyone else calm.

2. Be sure no one gets hurt.

3. End the situation as quickly as possible.

Guidelines

Work together
You never want to deal alone with a person who is potentially dangerous, even if it's a simple matter of letting someone else on the desk know you are going over "to talk to that guy who seems to be acting strange." All staff

should be aware of the potential danger any time we are dealing with someone acting in an erratic manner. I don't want to sound like we are working in a combat zone, but we have to realize that preparation and awareness save lives. If we think of every interaction like this as something potentially serious, we will be ready to respond in the rare cases when the situation actually becomes threatening.

Look for information that may be helpful
Is the patron wearing a medical alert bracelet? Slippers or clothes that may indicate a recent stay at a hospital or nursing home? This could indicate a mentally ill person who is skipping medication or having other problems. Are there any signs of drugs or alcohol? These signs include dilated pupils, slurred speech, erratic movements, smell of alcohol, and so forth. Be especially careful with any signs of drugs or alcohol. Behaviors may change quickly. Someone who is disruptive because he is singing may become angry and dangerous if asked to stop.

Never touch a patron
Even a friendly pat on the back could get an unexpected response in return.

Use space to your advantage
If you suspect someone may be dangerous, keep physical space between you and the patron. The circulation desk is usually good. If you are on the floor when someone presents a problem, sit the patron down at a table if possible. This not only puts space between you and the patron, but having you both sitting is a little calming. It is also harder for someone to make a physical attack.

Keep all dealing in plain sight
When someone is causing a disturbance at a desk, we may want to move away from the desk where other patrons are passing through. Although that is often helpful, we don't want to take anyone potentially dangerous to an office or any enclosed area.

Again, a table in the public area may be best. Be sure a coworker can see and is watching attentively. Besides the increased safety, this ensures there are witnesses in case an unbalanced person tries to claim library staff engaged in improper behavior.

Arrange signals in advance

If someone is upset, sometimes stating that you will call the police adds a needed dose of reality and improves the patron's behavior. This is especially true of a patron who has just gotten extremely upset over some library issue, such as a missing book. In other instances, you may want or need to call the police without letting the patron know. This is where teamwork comes in. Have a nickname for the police (or security guards if you have them). For example, nickname the police *Mr. Webb.* Then you can tell a coworker, "I'm not authorized to do what this gentleman needs. Could you see if Mr. Webb is around? I think he can take care of this." The coworker will know to get to a phone away from the patron and make an emergency call to the police.

Communicate with each other

If there is a patron who frequently gives you trouble, odds are the same patron is causing problems with other staff and possibly the public. Ask other staff about the person. It's as simple as, "Have you ever seen that guy who always comes in first thing in the morning, wearing the same blue baseball cap? He seems angry all the time, and I think he has made a few comments to patrons that seem to scare them. Have you noticed him?" If your coworkers have observed the same issues with the same person, it may be time to take preventive action. If other staff have not noticed any problem, they will now be alert and work with you to see if they confirm your observations.

Make a plan to deal with an identified problem

Once you've identified a problem, there are steps you can take that may head off future problems. Make arrangements to have some appropriate person talk to the patron about the problems he or she is causing. You may have the director or some other management person meet with the patron and explain which behaviors are prohibited and let the patron know that repeating these behaviors will result in banning from the library, criminal prosecution, or some other action. Make sure that the actions and consequences are clearly spelled out. It may be advisable to have a letter prepared and give that to the person, repeating the information shared in the meeting. Take notes of any meeting with the patron and have at least one other person in the meeting. Be sure to listen to any comments the person has and note those also. In some cases, the patron may point out some issue that causes or exacerbates his or her behavior (e.g., "I wouldn't get so mad if the guards didn't follow me around all the time"). As with any library patron, if he or she presents a reasonable complaint, discuss how you will address it. If the patron complains about something you have no reason to change, explain that also.

If the patron is someone who you think is dangerous, you may want to talk to the police and ask them to come in and talk to the person. It may be advisable to pull in someone from the social service field. If you suspect the person is mentally ill, contact a local organization and see if you can get a caseworker to assist.

Situation of the Day

Daniel came in regularly to the library and did considerable research, especially in the magazine section. He is about forty, tall, and dressed in a professional manner. In between his research, he liked to find female staff members who were alone at a desk or in the stacks and make extremely crude comments to them. He would ask personal comments and use the most vulgar language possible. He never actually threatened anyone, but he still made the employees feel uncomfortable and harassed. Finally, one of the women brought Daniel's behavior up to her supervisor. The supervisor asked other supervisors if anyone else had problems with this individual, and it was soon learned that he was doing this in most departments of the library. It was agreed that the next time he came into the library, the assistant director would be informed immediately and he would meet with this person.

Daniel was in the following day, and the assistant director came down to meet him. He told Daniel that he had to talk to him about some problems he had heard about. Daniel was given a copy of the library rules, and the section about "using profane or threatening language" was especially pointed out. He was told he was welcome to continue using the library for research, but he could not violate the rules or he would be banned from the library. The next day, Daniel came in and repeated his harassment of female staff. The assistant director and security were notified, and Daniel was thrown out of the library permanently.

In this example, which is based closely on a true story, the process ultimately succeeded, but a preventable problem went on too long. Too many people had to wake up and dread going in to work because it might have meant more of Daniel's mistreatment.

The key to ending this situation was the employee who finally went to her supervisor and alerted him to the problem. Because Daniel never caused any problem with any male employee, the supervisor had no way of knowing how bad Daniel had made working conditions for the female staff. Because he always approached staff when they were alone, even the other staff did not realize how many people he had harassed.

Establishing communication between staff, making a plan, and then following it made the difference.

Communicate with the patron carefully but decisively

Extra listening is important. If someone is on the verge, we want to gather as much information as we reasonably can before responding. Ask a few clarifying questions, or ask, "What can I do to help?" When you respond, be polite but firm.

Look for creative options to get the patron out of the building

Suggest options, all of which are acceptable to you. It's fine to expand your options, but be sure they are all acceptable. *Acceptable* here does not necessarily mean within your policies. If someone seems dangerous, let's not be too picky about the rules. If we have a rule against giving refunds for the copy machine and a patron is screaming about one bad copy, it's time to seriously consider an exception to the rule. If a dime gets someone out of the building who we feel is a threat, that's money well spent. In this case, you may say something such as "Okay, I understand that you are upset that the copy machine messed up your copy and took your last dime. It sounds like you really need that form copied. Here's what I can do this time. I can make a copy for you at no charge. That will give you the copy you need and then you will be finished with your business in the library today, correct?"

Our rules are so drilled into us that sometimes they trap us. Remember, the rules only exist to help us operate smoothly. When a rule makes life more difficult, then it's to nobody's advantage to follow it. Give yourself the leeway to find a creative solution to a dangerous situation. We can't break every rule any time a patron gets upset, but we have to weigh the value of the rule against the risk of enforcing it.

Just because we go around a rule to get out of a touchy situation doesn't mean we are done with the situation. In the case of the free copy, we may follow up if this is a patron we see again. The next time the patron comes in, for example, one should immediately alert a manager or a guard. Talk to the person about the recent problem, and go over the rules. It should be a calmer situation this time, allowing a little more discussion of what can and can't be done. As with the last case, clearly state that violating the rules can lead to removal and banning from the library.

The bottom line is that we act in favor of safety first, and all other policies are second. A distant second.

Don't hesitate to call the police

Sometimes we think, "I don't want to bother the police; this is probably nothing." It's important to factor in response time. Even if you have always had great response time with someone showing up in two or three minutes, you never know if you're calling when the police are short staffed, dealing with an emergency elsewhere, or for some reason not giving the usual quick response. The day when we count on a two-minute response might be the day it takes them seven minutes. Those extra few minutes can mean everything in a real emergency.

All employees must know they are authorized to call the police

In routine cases, it's fine to wait and have the branch manager, supervisor, or director call the police. If we think someone has been stealing books or we see graffiti in the men's room, usually we can wait and have someone from management handle the police report. That may not be the case with a problem patron. If we are faced with a patron who is growing increasing angry, belligerent, or threatening, waiting fifteen minutes until the supervisor gets back from lunch is risky. Supervisors need to let all of their staff know that they can call the police if it seems like there is a chance of danger to staff or patrons. If the police come and it turns out the patron has calmed down or left, that's fine. Better to be safe than sorry.

Summary

Most of our time in library life will not involve dangerous individuals. The vast majority of our patrons will be pleasant or, at worst, indifferent. A few will be rude and require that we rise above it. For the few who may present a truly dangerous situation, we have to be prepared. Planning for the worst, working together, and staying calm can make all the difference in these instances.

We've spent the last five chapters looking at general methods for dealing with problems. Controlling ourselves and controlling the situation form the starting place for all these situations. There are some specific problems we are likely to encounter at the library. Because we know they are on their way, let's prepare now. The next chapters cover some common patron issues in the library and approaches to make dealing with them manageable.

6

Dealing with the Mentally Ill

We're used to all kinds of people visiting our library, and after a while it takes a lot to rattle us. Yet those customers who shows signs of mental illness are still confusing and upsetting to even some of the toughest library veterans. What do you say to someone wandering around holding an animated conversation with no one? Or to the person who insists the government is using the library to collect his fingerprints?

We want to keep control in our libraries, and people with bizarre behaviors threaten that control. It is possible to work with most behaviors in a way that allows our library to function yet still permits the patron with mental illness to use the facility. Recognizing that you will likely encounter people with mental illnesses at your library, we can set some reasonable goals.

Goals

1. Increase your understanding of mental illness.
2. Learn effective methods of communicating with mentally ill people who are creating a disturbance in the library.
3. Protect staff and patrons in rare instances of possible violence.

Mental Illness

When we discuss mentally ill patrons, we are usually talking about the extreme cases, people who exhibit bizarre behaviors, disorganized thinking, or extreme paranoia. These cases represent only a small portion of people with mental illnesses. The vast majority are not even noticed by us. It may help to learn a little more about this large group of people.

Mental illness is a broad term used to cover a variety of afflictions where a person's thinking differs significantly from other people's. According to the American Psychiatric Association, up to fifty million Americans— more than 22 percent—suffer from a clearly diagnosable mental disorder in any given year. This means that their illnesses are significant enough to interfere with employment, attendance at school, or daily life. The symptoms and illnesses vary almost as widely as physical illnesses. Appendix 1 gives a brief look at some of the most common types of mental illnesses and their symptoms.

Many people won't show any outward signs of their illnesses, especially in our brief contact at the library. Counseling or medication or both allow more and more people to function normally in everyday society. These are the success stories and will not have any impact on our library life.

The people we have to concern ourselves with are those who are not getting treatment or are getting unsuccessful treatment, have quit taking their medication, or for some reason cannot control the symptoms of their illness. They may challenge even the most skillful library employee.

Because there are many types of mental illnesses, it is impossible to develop one sure method for dealing with every patron whose mental illness is disturbing the library. There are some general guidelines on communication and approaches that will usually help bring the situation under control. A few of our standard approaches apply. We only have to address the mentally ill patron if his or her behavior is breaking a rule or interfering with the ability of others to use the library. If there is a library issue, we want to deal with that and see if we can eliminate the disruptive behavior by taking care of the problem.

Guidelines

Stay calm

If someone is exhibiting signs of mental illness, the last thing needed is for him or her to pick up stress from you. That will just escalate the situation.

Speak in a direct, clear manner

The same conditions that cause the person's mental illness may make communication more difficult. You can help by staying focused and straightforward. Stay on one topic at a time.

Connect a behavior to a result

Instead of saying, "You aren't allowed to stare at people. It's against the library rules," try a different approach. "When you stare at people in the library, it makes them nervous and scared. They can't do their library work. Two people have said that they were leaving the library because they felt you were staring at them. The library considers staring to be harassing, and it is against library rules." This way the person knows that his or her behavior has had a consequence on other people. It's probably not necessary the first time you talk to a patron about this that you mention throwing him or her out of the library if he or she continues to stare. When we tell teenagers they are talking too loudly the first time, we don't usually tell them they will be removed if they don't quiet down. Treat this situation in the same manner, and save that warning for a second conversation if one is needed.

Offer options

With the staring patron, for example, you could offer to get him something to read. If he just wants to stare, tell him that he can turn a chair toward a wall or look out a window or leave the library.

Communicate rules and limits

Explain which behaviors are acceptable and which are not. Be specific. "It's fine if you look at our magazines. You can stay here as long as you like while you do this. It is not acceptable that you take every single magazine and pile them all up on a table to go through. When you do that, no one else can use them, and that's not fair. You can take two magazines at a time to your table. When you are done with those, return them and then you may take two more. You should never have more than two magazines at a time at your table. Do you understand this rule?" Be sure to share with other staff any agreements you have made with a patron so they know and can help enforce these agreements consistently.

Don't argue about another person's hallucinations

It won't do any good. The reality inside the person's head is too strong to be easily removed. Arguing will most likely produce stress and anger, and it may make you a target of hostility. Paranoia sometimes accompanies delusions and hallucinations, so arguing could lead the person to believe you are against him or her. Accept the person's perception, even if you know it is not true. You may need to acknowledge the patron's reality, but usually you don't need to play along. For example, if someone is carrying on a loud conversation with a person who is not there, you don't have to convince this person that there is no one there. All you have to do is reduce the noise.

Don't talk down to someone who is mentally ill

Mental illness does not mean a loss of intelligence any more than physical illness does. Treating a patron as less than intelligent may lead to anger or resentment, but it will not lead to cooperation.

Writing it down can help

People who are experiencing extremely disorganized thinking can be difficult to communicate with. They will not hear what you say the same way other people would. Sometimes writing down information helps. Other times, hand gestures and body language can get a point across. In a case this severe, keep your message as short and simple as possible. Don't deal with any details; just focus on presenting the problem and work to solve that.

Never make the person feel trapped or threatened

Nobody wants to feel like there is no way out, and that is especially true with a mentally ill person. There are a few specific ways to avoid creating these feelings. Sitting down when talking to someone who is sitting down seems less threatening. If the person is standing, sit and invite them to sit. It's friendly, professional, and actually is safer for you because it's harder to launch a physical attack when sitting, especially across a table. Don't stand between the person and the exit. Allow them to feel they can walk away easily if they wish. I knew one woman who enjoyed a support group I worked with, but one time she came in and immediately left. She told me later she could only be there if she had a chair by the door, and that time the chair was taken. She had to feel like she could leave, even if she never wanted to.

Beware of violence

The threat of violence from a person with mental illness does exist, but so does the threat from other non-mentally ill people. If we have fifty million people in America with some type of mental illness, it is obvious that the vast majority are not violent. However, we hear about the half a dozen per year and generalize that to this entire population. That is both unfair to this group of people and risky to us. Because most people who commit violent acts are not mentally ill, we should concern ourselves with the wider population for our own safety.

Some mentally ill people can be violent. The best predictor is past violent behavior, which may be difficult for us to know. Contacting the police or a social service worker with the mental health system might help find out about a certain individual. Attacking property is also considered a sign of possible violent behavior. Hurling books, breaking furniture, or pushing over displays are warning signs. Contact the police immediately.

The vast majority of people with mental illness will not pose a threat or even be noticed in our libraries. The few whose symptoms do cause a disturbance can usually be dealt with by using a combination of preparation, patience, clear communication, and understanding.

7

Anger in the Library

A display of anger in the library is one of the most troubling situations we can encounter. It brings fear of violence, it scares patrons of all ages, and it frightens many staff members, too. Anger brings a more emotional, gut reaction than most any other display of emotion; and responses can be anything from more anger to crying. How we respond depends on factors like our personal experience and our immediate concern for our safety.

There are a variety of reasons why we may find ourselves faced with an angry person at our library. Sometimes a library service didn't go right. A book is missing, the computer shows a fine on a book the patron swears she never had, or a staff member failed to provide the level of service the patron expected. Many times the person's anger has no relation to the library. It could be a confrontation between two patrons, a sign of drugs or mental illness, or an extremely bad day.

Anger Is a Secondary Emotion

Understanding anger can help us deal with it when confronted with an angry patron. The most important fact about anger is this: anger is a secondary emotion. What does that mean? Don't get mad; I was getting ready to explain. It simply means that anger springs from some other emotion. Think of times when you get angry. How about when you are running late for work and can't find your car keys? That's a good way to get me angry. What I'm really feeling is frustration and anxiety, but it's easier to express anger by yelling than to express frustration. We lash out because we don't know any other way to deal with what we are feeling.

Despite the fact that anger is a secondary emotion, it still is significant. An elevated temperature is a secondary effect of many diseases, but a prolonged, high temperature can have life-threatening effects of its own. That's why doctors often treat the fever while treating what is causing it.

In some ways, that's what we have to do when dealing with an angry patron. We have to handle both the anger and the root cause of the anger. How do we do that?

It's really a process, starting with basic steps that will calm down the average person and moving toward firmer action for those who remain not only angry, but disruptive and dangerous. Let's look at some goals and guidelines.

Goals

1. Protect the safety of staff and patrons.
2. Try to identify a cause of the anger and deal with the cause.
3. Attach consequences to continued disruptive behavior.
4. Summon the police if the anger threatens anyone.

Guidelines

Stay calm
Anger pushes our buttons, but responding in kind will just escalate the situation. Keep a moderate tone of voice (don't go extra soft—you'll sound patronizing and risk increasing the patron's anger). Don't take comments personally because that will make you angry, something you need to avoid.

Keep yourself out of danger
Never get in between two angry people. You weren't hired to be a bouncer.

Focus on the issue
If a library issue led to the display of anger, try to focus the discussion on it. It's important that the angry person feels like progress is being made toward solving the problem. That can go a long way toward diffusing anger. Sometimes

it's a problem you can't solve or a policy you can't change that is fueling the anger. For example, the patron wants to check out a reference book that doesn't go out. Obviously, you can't change library policy every time someone gets angry. In these cases, explain the policy; then check to see if there is another book or article that may satisfy this patron's need. Also explain that you cannot change the policy. That's up to the director or the board of trustees. Suggest the patron contact them to get this changed, and offer paper and pen if he or she would like to write a letter immediately.

Bring in someone else

If the patron has made you the target of his anger, you will have a tough time overcoming that. See if you can get another staff person to step in. It's hard to yell at someone you just met and who has yet to deny your request. A new start sometimes helps to return the focus to the issue at hand. If you are denying the patron something he feels he should not be denied (such as the reference book), it sometimes helps if the patron hears it from more than one person. This also reduces the odds of a person focusing his anger on one staff member, and gives him the policy to be angry at rather than the person who explained the policy. Additionally, the new person on the scene may add an idea that may help solve the dilemma.

Address the anger

In some cases, going through the above process will bring the decibel level back to the acceptable range. Unfortunately, not everyone will be calmed down easily. You will need to remind this patron to quiet down. Try a comment such as, "I'll do all I can to help you, but I need to ask you to lower your voice, please." Stay positive and focused on the issue, but let the patron know that he or she has to participate in the process also.

Another way to address the anger is to reflect the patron's feelings back to him or her. "I can tell this policy is making you upset." That shows you understand the impact this is having on the patron and builds a bit of a connection between the two of you. That connection can reduce any hostility the patron feels toward you personally, which is a good way to avoid violence. I prefer to say *upset* rather than *angry* because *upset* doesn't have the negative ring to it that *angry* does, and it also is a little broader, covering more of a range of emotions.

Attach consequences to continued disruptive behavior

You need to let the patron know that his or her actions are unacceptable and will not produce the desired results. Here you need to keep a positive, calm tone of voice, but you must also sound firm. Make eye contact. The patron needs to know this is a partnership, and you are going to do your share, but he or she needs to reciprocate. "I want to help you with this, but I can't unless you calm down, okay?" Or, "I'm willing to do everything I can to help, but if you continue to disrupt the library, I'll have to ask you to leave." In serious matters, you need to tell the patron you will call the police if the problem continues. Of course, you should never make any sort of statement like that if you do not intend to follow through.

These steps are more designed to deal with the results of the anger (yelling, threatening, disrupting the library, etc.). If someone is angry but keeps things under control, you certainly don't need to take any steps to address that anger. It's only when it flares out of control that you need to take action.

Being around anger is stressful. If you stay calm and deal with the root cause, you are a long way toward getting out of this unpleasant situation.

8

What to Do about Suspected Child Abuse

Working on the front lines of a public library, you'll encounter all kinds of people and situations. Most are enjoyable or at least not bad. A few are horrible, and none may be more difficult than seeing a case of suspected child abuse. It may be a crying child dragged by one arm, a spanking that goes well beyond behavior modification, or overhearing cruel, insulting, and hurtful words.

These scenes present a real dilemma to the library staff. Is there anything you can do? Ignoring it is difficult—making us feel guilty, worried about the child, and aware that other library patrons are watching. Getting involved is even harder—what can you do to help? Will that make life harder for the youngster? Are you putting yourself or others in danger?

Personally, maybe more than any other situation, I wish there were a simple answer to share. Although there is no magic answer, there are some options to keep in mind.

Goals

1. Avoid making anything worse.
2. Don't risk the safety of library staff or patrons.
3. Know when to intervene and some possible ways to help.

Guidelines

Usually, we do not get involved

In most of the cases we see, it's better not to step in. Emotionally, it is difficult as human beings to sit back and watch someone helpless being mistreated. The sad fact is that a parent who is harsh and cruel with a child in public is most likely as bad or worse at home. Intervening may embarrass the parent and result in more anger being directed toward the child.

Get involved only if you can help

Sometimes help is welcomed. For example, an overstressed mother may appreciate a sincere and appropriate offer of help. This is the mom who may have several preschool children, and one of them is crying while the other keeps asking, "Mom, when are we going to get my books?" Or it could be a father who needs to get something for himself and the children aren't allowing that task to be completed. In times like this, it's easy to get frustrated and angry, lashing out at the kids. We might be able to provide a little assistance in these situations.

On the other hand, a mother having a showdown with her youngster may see another person as interfering and preventing her from establishing her authority. She may direct her anger at the staff person and then resume the feud with her child at home.

The best way to help is to be sympathetic and positive

If there is a time when you feel you can do some good for parent and child, then it may be worthwhile to get involved. Here's an example:

> A young mother is in the children's room with two youngsters, one about two and the other about a few months old. The youngest is crying, probably needing a diaper change. As the mother tries to haul both into the rest room, the two-year-old throws a fit, refusing to move. Mom tries dragging him by the arm, and he gets louder, yelling in both pain and anger. Meanwhile, Mom is losing her composure as the infant adds her voice to the chorus. Others in the room watch uncomfortably as the situation grows louder and uglier.
>
> Approach with a few picture books in hand. Smile and say, "You have a real handful there. Would it help if I read to him while you take her into the bathroom?"
>
> "I don't know if he's going to let anyone move him. He's stubborn when he wants to be," says Mom.

"Well, we don't really need to move him. I can sit right by him and read to him here. What's his name?" you ask.

"Tommy," says Mom.

"Tommy, which one of these books do you like the best? Can you point to one?" you ask, taking a seat on the floor next to him and holding up two books. Tommy stops crying long enough to give a halfhearted point to one of the books. From there you can engage him in the book and free up Mom long enough for her to accomplish her mission. She should explain to Tommy, "Stay here with the librarian, and I'll be right back."

Although we don't want to start a baby-sitting service, this type of help may be the only way to prevent a child from getting hit.

Other types of help might include getting books the family is looking for while she attends to the kids or looking up her card number so she doesn't have to try to fish out her library card while everything else is going on. Sometimes the best approach is to simply ask what help she can use. For example, "Kids can really be a handful. What can I do to help?" It may take a little talking and prompting to get an answer. She may have to tell you a little about why she's at the library and what the problem is before you can get to problem solving. As you listen, see if you can suggest a way to help.

Simply walking up to the parent and offering assistance is helpful even if you don't end up giving any actual help. It pulls the parent out of where she is and gives a little break. It also provides a gentle reminder that the situation is going on in public and is possibly getting more attention than the parent wants. When we realize our actions are being observed, most people try to be sure that those actions are not anything that will embarrass us.

Get outside help

If a situation looks like real child abuse, well beyond a stressed parent showing frustration and poor judgment, then it may be necessary to intervene in ways other than talking to the parent. There are several possibilities, depending on your community. The most universal option is to call the police. This should only be considered when the treatment of the child is severe and it looks like things will continue to escalate. A good police officer will know how to intervene, talking to the parent rather than looking to arrest someone. Just the presence of the uniform and authority will usually stop the current abuse.

Most communities have child abuse prevention agencies. If your library staff feel that this child abuse in the library is a concern, have someone from this agency come out and discuss their programs. Find out how they would respond if you called and said, "I think there is a little child being abused in the library. Can you help?" What services do they offer, and are there other agencies we should know about? They may be able to provide some guidance on handling difficult situations and even offer training for the staff. If you do get information from this agency, be sure all staff know how to use this service.

In extreme cases, you may want to call the police or your children's protection agency after the family leaves. Some localities allow anonymous reporting of suspected child abuse. *Be extremely careful.* I am the world's biggest bleeding heart, especially when it comes to children. Thinking about a child getting hurt is one of the worst things in the world for me, and many other people feel the same way. However, reporting a family from the library may involve the library in the future. That raises some significant questions:

> Do we break our patron confidentiality policy to get information for the police? I have heard some argue that it's acceptable because our confidentiality only covers what the patron checks out, and we are not revealing this. Others disagree. It is a slippery slope and one your library needs to carefully consider.

> What if we know the patron and give the name without using our records? That may be safer but as long as you saw something to report at the library, there is a chance the library will become involved. It's the same if you get the license plate number of the parent's car. There's still a chance that the library will end up involved.

> Who decides? If the family leaves and the treatment of the children was abusive and you have reason to suspect that more abuse is going on, are you the person who should make the decision to call the authorities? Your supervisor? The director? The board?

When you see a family leaving the library and you think there is reason to believe that the child will be abused at home, that's the wrong time to get into a legal and philosophical debate. At that point, there's too much emotion and not enough time. Have this discussion *before* a crisis. Sit down with some staff and discuss the options and ramifications. Get legal advice regarding laws in your community and find out about the reporting procedures. If you make a decision to give out patron information in cases where it seems a child may be in danger, be sure all staff understand the circumstances and procedures for handling this delicate matter. You should have a written procedure for these situations that has been reviewed and approved by your legal authority and governing body.

Be sure you know the laws regarding child abuse and reporting potential neglect. In most cases, librarians are not required to notify anyone of suspected abuse the way a teacher or doctor may be. Generally, our requirement is more moral than legal.

9

Taming the Internet

Progress is a great thing. It just went on too long.

—James Thurber

For libraries, the proof of progress going on "too long" is the Internet. This new technological wonder offers more access to information than any invention in history. It also offers more new problems. When we introduced videos into our library, they attracted some new customers and introduced some new issues. We weren't sure we would survive at first. This new technology was more complicated than books. The people who came in just for videos were often more demanding than we were used to, and they were not always familiar with the way a library worked. They treated us like video store operators, but they generally came and left fairly quickly. We've learned and adapted, and, for the most part, loaning videos is not much more difficult than loaning books.

Will we be as successful with the Internet? The new audience the Internet attracts often stays and stays. The technology is much more complex, and many library staff members don't understand it. The media hype has encouraged a growing group of novice users to investigate what this thing is, and these newbies often start at their public library. When we mix them with the Internet fanatics and a staff struggling to understand what we have here, the situation is "dynamic," to put it nicely.

What new challenges does the Internet pose? Three main issues exist:

1. Sharing the resource in demand with all those who want to use it

2. Providing assistance to users unfamiliar with the technology, despite the fact that staffing is already short and not all library personnel have adequate knowledge

3. Addressing the controversial material available

Only three issues concern us, but plenty of potential questions and headaches can accompany them. Let's go through them one at a time.

Dealing with Our Popularity

Basically, we have too many people wanting to use too few machines. Most libraries do not have enough computers available no matter how many they actually have. This is especially true at the after-school crunch time. Additionally, a few users will spend all day, if possible, on the computer. (Where is carpal tunnel syndrome when you need it?) Just a few of these folks can tie up precious computer resources all day, frustrating staff, and generating complaints from other would-be users. They also discourage the casual users or the person who hasn't used the Internet before from trying. It's amazing how many problems a couple of people can cause, but if your library has only a few Internet computers, and two or three regulars who like to spend all day, you've got little availability for other users.

Set Time Limits

How do we allow these regulars to use the computer but still make space for the others? The most common method is time limits—thirty minutes to one hour at a time. Essentially, we've created a loan period for an in-house item. That's a reasonable and often necessary approach. The real question is how to implement this time limit. There is no one preferred method because different libraries have different resources and needs. Here's a brief look at some of the common methods and the pros and cons.

Methods of Enforcing Computer Use Time Limits

	Disadvantages	Advantages
Enter Library Card	Problem for those who forget card Requires a little more skill from user Requires more technology Denies non-card-holding patrons	Less staff time on a regular basis Know user is a card holder May help track use
Honor System	Violated by troublemakers Without a written start time, can lead to disputes	Lowest staff time
Sign In	Requires constant staff involvement Sign-in sheets could be public record	Allows fairness and close monitoring May require card
Advance Registration	Demands on patron No shows	Convenience for those who plan Staff know what to expect

There are a few other twists to the time limits. One library sets a kitchen timer to go off when the time limit is reached. This frees staff from the unpleasant duty of tapping a patron on the shoulder. There's another innovative and somewhat quieter approach. When a patron signs in for his thirty minutes, he is given an index card with his ending time written in large print. This is placed on top of the computer in a special holder, and the whole world (or least anyone interested) knows at what time this computer will become available.

Get More PCs!

Don't rule out acquiring more computers. We see our budgets and think it's all we can do to afford the few we currently have. Donations from businesses, computer clubs, or civic groups or other organizations are strong possibilities. The easiest donation to get is for specific, one-time purchases, and that's just what you are looking for. Offering to put a sign "Donated by the Springfield Elks Club" on the computer can really help. Be picky about accepting donations of used computers. If they are outdated, in need of repair, or incompatible with your other equipment, the gift may be more hassle than it's worth. Asking for money is less enjoyable than a root canal, but if it reduces some of the backlog on the Internet waiting list, it will be worth it in the long run (again, just like that root canal!).

Set Daily Limits for Internet "Addicts"

Many libraries report that they have a few people who spend their lives on the computer. If they have to get off because of time limits, they immediately sign up again and impatiently wait for their next turn. If this is a problem, try setting a daily limit for individuals. If you have a thirty-minute limit when people are waiting, there's no reason you can't set a three-hour-per-day limit for any person. Few people would have trouble with a limit of two or three hours per day. Only the real Internet "addict" will be affected. Time limits could apply only during busy times, not when you have lots of open computer time, for example, in the mornings.

A time limit for an individual may mean you will occasionally have a computer empty while your favorite Internet addict is without a computer to use. That's not unlike a limit on how often one person can renew a book, a rule many libraries have. If I am the only person around who wants the book *The Joys of Cataloging*, I may believe I should be able to renew it for years at a time. I would argue that if someone wants it, he or she can put a reserve on it and then he or she can have it. However, we know not everyone will place reserves, so most libraries require that the book spend a little time on the shelf. This isn't really different from the time limit for individuals. We know that some curious patrons may sit down and try the Internet if they see computers available, but these same patrons may not go through the sign-up process if they see the computers in use all the time. Creating a daily limit for each person allows more people an opportunity to experiment and reduces the monopoly problem a few people can create.

Those few people who want to live on your computers will probably complain about a daily limit. Explain it as you would a limit on renewal of books—that it is a way to be sure everyone gets to share these public resources. They still may be unhappy but that's fine. Library vandals may not appreciate our rule against vandalism, but that's unlikely to get us to eliminate that rule. Our goal on this, and other policies, is to satisfy the average, reasonable person. We'll never make the extremes happy nor should that be our target. Folks who want to spend all day on the machine will disagree with any limit, and those who won't use them could care less.

Helping with Technology; or, I Can't Find the "Any Key!"

If you don't know the story behind the "any key," you should. According to surveys, the most commonly asked question to technical support telephone help lines is: "It says to hit any key to start, but I can't find the any key."

Even if you know how to find any key, giving assistance on accessing the Internet can be a real source of stress for staff and the public. Ideally, we would add staff when we add Internet-accessible computers—people to help customers use their new equipment. Sometimes present staff can absorb the extra work into the regular schedule, but often more assistance is needed. We add shiny new computers but seldom add staff to help the public with them. So people want to use them, get confused and frustrated, and demand staff help, but staff cannot leave their other areas to help. The result? Stress all around.

If we want to avoid unhappy patrons, we have to find a way to offer some assistance while still living within our budgets. A few approaches follow:

Use volunteers
The computer world generates lots of loyal people, and that gives us a large pool from which we can recruit volunteers. Computer clubs, businesses, and stores attract enough to give us a good supply. It's important that these volunteers be carefully trained on basic policy, confidentiality, and exactly how to help. They will know the Internet operations pretty well, but we do have to show them any special library services and make them aware of our rules.

Offer training classes
This won't meet an immediate need but will help you if a patron needs more assistance than you can give at that moment. It's also good publicity. Be sure you have a general outline, and anyone who teaches these classes should follow the same basic outline. These classes give us a chance to explain all our cool new policies, but that's not why the people are there. Give enough information to handle any major issues, such as time limits, and have handouts to go into a bit more detail.

Let the patrons help each other
It actually happens frequently, if your setup allows it. Place several Internet-accessible computers together, with some kind of barrier or privacy screen for confidentiality. Patrons will share what they know and often give the answers to basic operation questions and even recommend sites.

Create instruction sheet
Most libraries create some form of written guidelines for using the Internet-accessible computer. This can be helpful, but we have to accept that many people cannot get started by written instructions alone. No matter how simple the written instructions are, human assistance will be needed for some.

Some combination of these steps, plus stealing as much time as possible from other duties, will at least provide a start for most people. Like any other patron issue, if we demonstrate that we are trying to help, that goes a long way toward avoiding conflict. Referring patrons who need extra help to a class or a time when a volunteer will be on-site also avoids making them feel abandoned or disrespected, feelings that can lead to conflict.

Dealing with Controversial Material and Other Fun Topics

Another big aspect of the Internet challenge is the "free access versus protecting children" argument. Part of how we gain control of this situation is with the set-up of our computers. Do we put them in a highly visible area, which will reduce the instances of patrons displaying graphic sexual images on the screen but will still result in an uproar? Do we tuck the computers away in a corner and decide that what we can't see can't hurt us? Do we instruct staff to tell patrons displaying sexual images to stop looking at that site? Or do we tell patrons who complain about seeing these images when they walk by with a grandchild that the viewer has the right to look at anything he or she wishes?

Currently, one of the most major decisions you will have to make is regarding the use of filtering software. As you most likely know, this software is designed to block Web sites that contain objectionable materials. Like everything else, this software is far from perfect. While we may employ it to block sites with graphic sexual images, it will sometimes block sites about birth control, sex education, or breast cancer. It will also sometimes allow access to sites that it is expected to block. With millions of Web sites and things changing by the second, there is no way that any software can perform perfectly. One side says to use it and at least block some of the problem sites. The other point of view maintains that installing this software can give parents a false sense of security and lead them to expect the library to handle the problems.

If you decide to use blocking software, your decision making is not finished. Most software gives you a choice on what types of sites you want to block. You need to decide if you want to block sites with violence, sex, nudity, cigarettes, beer, bomb-making, or some combination of these. Also, you have to decide if you will use blocking software on all computers or just the ones for children. Libraries using the software on all computers have been found in violation of the First Amendment. If you just want to use blocking software for children, you have to determine how to do that. Do you have separate computers for adults and for kids? What do you do when the computers for kids are all in use and the ones for adults are idle and several children are waiting to use the Internet?

There is a compromise available on the question of blocking for everyone or just for minors. When schools use blocking software in the classroom, they often have a password to allow the teacher to bypass the block if needed. That software may be modified for libraries. For example, at the Dayton, Ohio, library there is blocking software on all Internet computers. If a site is blocked that an adult wants to go to, the adult can enter her library card number. The computer checks this with the library's database and if the card number belongs to an adult, then the filtering software is bypassed. It's still not a perfect solution because kids can enter a card number of an adult and get around the software. It also requires someone with good technical skills to set up and maintain. Other libraries allow minors to use the Internet only with written permission from parents.

It may be simpler to skip the blocking software and allow unlimited access but this approach comes with its own set of complications. We have to be prepared to deal with the angry parent who wants to know why the library allowed his child to print pictures of graphic sexual images from the screen. The net offers pictures of everything you can imagine and lots of things you can't. The curiosity and persistence of youngsters mean that they are likely to try to explore the dark side of the Internet. So what happens when a child is caught selling pictures at school that he printed at the library? What if this is three weeks before your levy?

Libraries have been sued both for filtering and for not filtering. It will be years, if ever, before there is clear direction from the courts. Meanwhile, the debate on filtering versus unlimited access will continue to rage (and in many cases rage is not an overstatement). We have to accept that whatever decisions we make on access issues, some people will be unhappy.

With that in mind, let's look at the people aspect. Whatever side of the filter/nonfilter debate your library ends up on, there's a good chance that some people in your community (and even in your library) will disagree. Dealing with the communication issues now can help prevent problems if disagreements arise later.

Create an Internet Policy

The first layer of protection is a carefully designed policy that not only sets forth how your library will handle Internet use but also some whys behind the decisions. Think about your library's purpose and staff setup. Consider your community and your library's relations with the community. What does the community expect? Need? Have they been active? If so, in what way? What do your funders expect? What action or inaction will cause the most problems? Are there other players in this such as schools, day cares, and others?

You may want to review Internet policies from other libraries. There are many available on the Web. (See also appendix 2 for some sample Internet policies.) It's especially useful to see what areas they address to determine if you have overlooked an important policy issue. All libraries are not the same, however, so don't feel like you should have to include everything other policies cover. Before adding a section, ask yourself, "Is this something we are likely to face?" If not, leave it out. You can always go back and add to your policy, so don't feel like it has to be perfect and address every possible issue.

Like other policies, these must be simple, clear, and readable. Your policy must be easily explained by staff to anyone, and the explanation must be understood. It's a little harder to keep Internet policies on the easy-to-read level, because of its newness and complexity. We don't understand it, we don't know what could happen, so we better make a policy about it. Instead of cluttering up your policy statement with pages of details and things that could happen, add a general statement to cover unknowns, such as "Any action that alters or damages the computer or interferes with other people's ability to use the computer is prohibited."

Jargon is also a barrier to creating clear policies. There are so many technological terms that can easily slip into the rules and really not be understood. Have a few nontechnical people read the draft policies and see if they can understand them. You may have to use a more general term or define the jargon within the policy document.

Like other policies, the development of these should involve all staff who interact with the public and the Internet, including children's librarians, reference librarians, and technology staff.

After you have the policy, you should get a legal review to be sure that it doesn't violate any local ordinances or omit anything. As with legal reviews of any policy, work with your attorney to prevent your readable document from being translated into legalese. Then have your board or governing body approve the policy. Because they are unlikely to be familiar with all the Internet issues, take extra time to ensure they understand what they are approving. Bring your board up-to-date on the questions Internet accessibility in the library raises, the responses you have chosen, and the reasoning behind your decisions. Be sure you explain what you didn't do as well as what you did do. Chances are, they may not know all of the questions to ask, so go the extra mile to inform them. The advantage of a board-approved policy is that it insulates the staff to some degree from any criticism from the public. If they approve a policy without understanding all the issues, you essentially lose that advantage because they are unlikely to be active in supporting a policy they didn't understand. The extra time spent giving your board all the background they need will be worth it if there ever is a public debate.

Inform the Internet Users

The next step is to inform the public about the Internet-use policy. This includes giving handouts to the public, posting it on your Web site, and even sending out a news release. Normally, new policies are not a good subject for a news release, but this can be worked into a story about the new service and how the library is handling it. Like everything else with Internet use, informing the public seems a bit more complicated, perhaps because so many people don't know much about it. We need to be simple and concise or no one will read our information. On the other hand, we need to explain the issue thoroughly enough that anyone can understand, which may mean more description.

We have to look for the legendary middle ground here and hope it exists. Our main handouts and news releases can hit the highlights of the policy, the issues that will impact people the most. Time limits, scheduling, printing, and filtering information may be the topics for a simple handout. This would end by stating, "A complete policy is available at the library or online at www.dewey.library.org". We can then have another handout with the complete policy available near the computer, posted on our Web site, and otherwise handy in the library. This way we can produce a handout that is brief enough so most people will read it yet still contains all the details necessary to cover a complex issue such as the Internet.

The public will generally accept the fact that this technology is new and constantly evolving, and we still don't know exactly what the questions are, much less the answers. They will only accept that, however, if we can show we are working steadily to address issues as they arise and are taking a responsible, proactive stance. Developing policies, training staff and the public, and getting the word out are good starts.

It will take time to tame this electronic beast known as the Internet. We tamed videos and other new services, so that offers us hope. On the other hand, it has been 4,000 years and no one has truly been able to domesticate the cat.

10

Talkative People

They don't threaten you or your patrons. They just threaten your sanity. Those often friendly, well-meaning sorts who go on and on, unaware of your job duties. One of the nice aspects about working at a library is meeting people. However, we usually don't have time for in-depth conversations with them.

Most of the people who take up your time talking are obviously lonely. They usually love books and may have a subject or hobby they are extremely interested in but lack people to share their interest. Going to the library may be the one contact with other people in their long day. A few show various degrees of mental illness, ranging from being just a little confused to behaving very bizarrely. Regardless of the cause, we still have other patrons to help, books to shelve, and a thousand other duties, none of which get done while we are being talked to. We have to put some limits on our time, no matter how sweet the talker is.

How do we do that politely but firmly? That's the challenge. As a first step, most of us will try, "Gee, that's really interesting. I have to get back to work now." The friendly break doesn't always work, so we need another escape route. Following are a few options:

Put as much physical distance as possible between you and the talker
If you are shelving in the stacks, tell the patron you have to get back to the workroom. Then, head to a back area where the public is not allowed. Behind the desk, you may be able to move to the other side of the desk, but if that doesn't work, you will have to duck into a nonpublic area.

Use a little teamwork
If you see your coworker stuck and he or she is near a phone, call from a back office. Quietly let your coworker know what you are doing and stay on the line until the patron leaves. A similar approach is to walk up to your stuck coworker and say that he or she has a long-distance phone call in the back. The long-distance element adds a touch of urgency.

Do some preparation
Arrange signals such as a tug of the ear to let your coworkers know it's time for a phone call. Most of our talkers are regulars and recognizable, so we can plan for them. You and your coworkers decide that when that talkative lady who gets all the quilting books comes by, someone will rescue you a minute or two after she finishes checking out.

It's harder if you're alone and trapped behind the desk. Again, the telephone is your best bet. Tell the talkative person that you promised you would call someone at a given time. Pick up the phone and dial time and temperature until your person wanders off.

Give referrals
You can also try a more positive approach. If the talkative person is really lonely and has a specific interest, you might refer them to a club or organization. Any organization—from a book discussion club to the local gardening society—might give them a place to find some companionship.

No matter how much we like our friendly talkers, we do have to move them to get our work done.

11

The Homeless in the Library

One of the most common patron concerns in libraries is the homeless. It's not just an issue for big urban libraries either. Small-town libraries and even affluent suburban libraries are facing this situation. People who need a place to go flock to libraries. Why not? We're ideal. Who else offers comfortable chairs, convenient location, free reading materials, rest rooms, water fountains, an escape from the elements, and no one trying to get you to buy anything? It's perfect.

Who Are They? Why Are They Here?

Any good marketing person will tell you to study your customer base, and because the homeless are part of our base, it's worth a quick look to find out a little about them. America's homeless problem has been growing steadily since the 1960s. Between 1960 and 1984, the population of the nation's mental health facilities decreased from 544,000 to 134,000. Many of the people released from these facilities lacked jobs and social skills as well as family support, making them prime candidates for life on the streets.

In the 1980s, approximately one-half million mentally ill people were removed from the welfare rolls, adding to the number of people at risk to end up on the streets. How many actually did is anybody's guess. Counting the homeless seems impossible. Results of studies vary widely, ranging from 300,000 to 3 million nationally. Typically, estimates are of 600,000 to 700,000 on any given night.

Whatever the number is, the groups can be divided into two distinct categories. The *crisis homeless* are people who have been forced from their homes and will immediately start looking for work or a new place to live. This group includes abused women, people who can't pay the rent because of losing a job, or those suffering from other economic hardships. Sadly, children are increasingly becoming part of this group. The good news is that they have a decent chance of finding some sort of living arrangement. Improvement for the other group is less likely. They are the *chronic homeless*, and these are who we usually see in the library. They are the hard core of the homeless population, often with drug-abuse and mental-illness histories.

A recent government report gives a good look at the characteristics of the entire homeless population. Single, unattached adults make up 75 percent of the population, and families with kids are about 20 percent.

The average age of these adults is in the thirties and the group is disproportionately minority. Three-quarters have spent time in some kind of institution, whether it is jail, a residential mental health facility, or a rehab center. To no one's surprise, at least half have alcohol or drug-dependency problems, and one-third have severe mental illness. Physical health ailments are also uncommonly high, with AIDS and tuberculosis especially prevalent. Only about half have completed high school. A surprising fact researchers notice but can't really explain is the high rate of the homeless who spent some of their childhood in foster care. Twice as many women as men were likely to have lived in foster homes. About 40 percent of people living on the street are military veterans, many from the Vietnam era.

Clearly this is a population that faces a number of significant barriers. For a while the theory was "affordable housing will solve the homeless problem." Repeated failures with this approach demonstrated that housing alone is not enough. Programs that have been successful combine drug and mental health counseling, education, job-readiness training, and other support services with low-cost housing. Long-term involvement is usually required because people facing so many challenges are unlikely to live independently without a great deal of transition assistance.

What to Do with Three Million Campers

When we look at all the problems that come with this group and how they challenge the most skilled social workers, it is no wonder that libraries can have a tough time with them. Because we like to think of ourselves as something other than a free hotel, we often find ourselves at odds with our homeless patrons. What we want to do as a library and what the homeless need are worlds apart. Customers complain about the shabby appearance. They bring in big bundles of strange-looking items and leave them lying around. They sit for hours at the table, sometimes reading but often staring blankly into space. Sometimes the stare isn't so blank, focusing on a patron or staff member and causing that person great discomfort, even driving some patrons to leave without finishing their library business. And that doesn't even begin to touch on the other strange and disquieting habits displayed in the library, anything from talking loudly (to no one in particular) to pacing around endlessly. The single biggest complaint most libraries report about the homeless patrons is the smell. There's no use talking around it. Patrons can't work around the odor when it's severe, and staff need to take frequent breaks to get fresh air. It's a sad fact but one we can't ignore.

Because we can't ignore this situation, let's look at ways to address it.

Goals

1. Treat everyone fairly and in the same manner.
2. Ensure that the library is a safe and comfortable place to be for everyone.

Guidelines

Start with the proper policies

The first step is the library's "Rules of Conduct," the same policies that apply to everyone else. It's not legal or ethical to create rules that only apply to one class of people. That means when we write our general rules, we have to keep any problems with the homeless in mind and be sure our rules cover those situations. Most public libraries do this to some extent. I doubt that corporate libraries have rules against sleeping in the library, and there may even be times when the weary executive gets some shut-eye while trying to complete a research project. We have the sleeping rule in public libraries mostly because of the possibility of homeless turning the library into a real hotel. Our rule is legal and ethical because it applies to everyone, even if we did create it specifically to deal with the homeless issue.

When writing these rules, we need to focus on the behavior we are concerned about, and not focus on any certain group. If you are writing rules because of issues with homeless patrons, start by making a list of all the behaviors that cause complaints from staff and patrons. Ask the frontline staff to give their input. That's the easy part. Now that you have your list, try to come up with specific prohibitions against those behaviors. For some, such as sleeping, it will be easy. For others, such as "acting crazy," it will take more work. What is it about acting crazy that causes a problem in the library environment? Talking loudly to oneself? Chances are you already have a rule against noise or loud conversation, so that rule can apply equally to a one-person conversation. How about staring? If a person is staring into space, that shouldn't be a problem. If a person is staring at staff or patrons in a way that makes them feel uncomfortable, that can qualify as harassment. Most libraries have rules against harassing behavior, so you should be able to stop that from happening with the antiharassing rule. Again, no separate rule is needed. If you don't have a rule prohibiting harassing behavior, it would make sense to develop one anyway. Patrons have the right to come to their library without fear of being harassed, and every library should have a rule that specifically prohibits any intimidating actions.

The smell issue is difficult. I'm not sure if it technically qualifies as a behavior, but it is a legitimate issue. Libraries' rules around the nation use phrases such as "sanitary or health risk," "offensive hygiene," "emanating an odor that can be detected six feet away," and "body odor." However we define it, perhaps the best approach is to base any action on the complaints of others patrons. Rules prohibiting such problems as "offensive body odor that prevents other patrons from using the library" are consistent with the reason we create rules in the first place—to help us operate a safe, efficient center for providing information to the public. Any behavior that interferes with our mission can reasonably be prohibited. Complaints from patrons offer some evidence that the odor is actually preventing people from using a library as a library is intended to be used.

Enforce rules in a fair, firm, and consistent manner

We need our rules to be respected and followed and that means acting against those who refuse to obey the rules. Because there aren't many library jails, our action is typically removing the offender from the library for some period of time. As a tax-supported, government institution, that removal is serious and can bring a lawsuit. Even if our rules are reasonable and legal, we still can be in trouble if we don't enforce them properly. The key is the same as in writing rules: we must focus on the behavior, not the person. That means that we wake up businesspeople who fall asleep doing research just as we would wake up a homeless person who is sleeping in the library. We have a rule against sleeping in the library, and we will enforce it, no matter who violates it. If we get lazy and only enforce the rule when we really feel like it, if some staff enforce but others don't, if we only enforce it against selected individuals, then we are at risk for a successful lawsuit. That's one of the reasons training is so important. All staff must know the rules and what their role is in enforcing them. If you hire guards, they also need to be trained and monitored to be sure they are treating every rule violator the same.

A consistent, progressive approach works best. First, let the person know he is breaking a rule. The second time, tell him that he has been warned once and if it happens again he will be asked to leave the library. At the third violation, he has to be told to leave. You can never make idle threats. Word-of-mouth communication is effective in the homeless population. If your library gets a reputation as a place where the rules can be easily ignored, your problems will multiply. If you make a rule, enforce it consistently and fairly.

Could your library be sued for removing someone due to odor? Sure. We can be sued for anything, and we simply have to accept that fact. Responding to complaints is probably the most solid legal footing libraries can achieve in this vague area. We are always at risk when any subjective judgment is required, but our best bet is to take our risks on behalf of people wanting to use us as a library. We can't let fear of a lawsuit prevent us from functioning as a library. All we can do is develop reasonable rules to protect our patrons and allow us to pursue our mission, obtain good legal advice in advance of approving our rules, and then enforce our rules in a fair, consistent manner. After that, if we get sued, then we hope our lawyer is better than their lawyer.

Involve social services

There are a number of ways we can provide some assistance to the homeless population at the library. One easy approach is to create a list of social services available, including counseling, traveler's aid, food, emergency shelter, job programs, medical services, and so forth. Besides using information at the library, work with organizations for the homeless to collect the information. Put all the numbers together on one piece of paper, preferably one that can fold down, pocket-size, for convenience. Staff should have a good supply of these. If you employ guards, they should also have a ready supply. If you can possibly afford it, print some extra copies for other concerned organizations to pass out.

Typically, most communities have a network of organizations assisting the homeless. There are usually several large core groups and a number of smaller organizations. Because funding is so tight, services and organizations can disappear and reappear quickly. It's hard to keep current, so many libraries find it useful to build strong ties with these groups. They can advise you on the latest services and options available. It may even be possible to borrow someone from these agencies to come to the library and help, especially with unusually difficult situations.

The homeless and public libraries are going to be together for the foreseeable future. We have to make the best of it. That is best done by developing policies that are fair to the homeless as well as other patrons, then enforcing these rules in a just and consistent manner. Practically and morally, we should do what we can to help people whose lives are in such desperate straits. That means connecting them with social services. It also means exercising the maximum tolerance possible. We have to draw the line, however, when a behavior interferes with the ability of others to use the library for its intended purpose. We have to act to stop the behavior that is interfering with others, but we can remember the difficulties in the life of a homeless person and act with compassion as well.

12

Hey, Lady! You Forgot Your Kids!

Never raise your hand to a child. It leaves your midsection unprotected.

—Robert Orben

Our libraries spend a tremendous amount of time and energy attracting and serving children. Maybe the only thing we spend more time and energy on is complaining about children at the library. Although we refuse to act in the role of parents, we sound like a parent with our "We love kids!" and "The kids are driving me crazy!" attitude.

For the most part, we are truly pleased when our facilities bustle with children exploring, reading, and learning. Whether they are listening to a toddler story time, finding books for Summer Reading Club, or doing that report on autumn leaves, we see kids at our library and know they are the future, both for our library and our nation. Nothing touches our hearts like the sight of a six-year-old sitting in a quiet corner, engrossed in the same Dr. Seuss book we read at that age. It's why most of us want to be in the library world.

Like any parent will happily point out, it's not all warm fuzzies around these little people. They have too much energy to sit quietly for long, and sitting quietly is what librarians like best. They haven't necessarily learned all our rules nor do they seem interested in making that effort. We put up all kinds of informative signs and alarmingly few nine-year-olds even bother to read them. Despite all the fine books we purchase and attractively display, some twelve-year-olds would rather giggle with each other than open even one BabySitter's Club title. The six-year-olds are more interested in the elevators than the award-winning dinosaur picture books, and we don't even want to know what interests the fifteen-year-olds. We can offer the best books and most entertaining, enlightening programs in the world, and youngsters will often choose some other way to find fun at the library. It's like the parents who spent their last dollar on that special birthday present to please their beloved child only to see the child play for hours with the box it came in. Welcome to the real world of kids. They have their own agenda and it may or may not overlap with ours.

That's where much of the challenge comes in for libraries. We know intellectually and emotionally that we want and need youngsters to come here and develop that all-important library habit. It will help them in school and for the rest of their lives. However, their energy, short attention spans, and willful spirit to follow their own interests don't always blend smoothly with the atmosphere of a library. We need a level of quiet below what is accepted on the playground to serve our adult patrons (and even many of our young ones). We have to enforce a certain number of rules to ensure good service for our wide variety of customers. The mix of youthful energy into this relatively quiet environment leads to plenty of headaches, no matter how strong our desire to serve this young population.

Lets look at the issues we face in addressing the challenges of mixing kids and adults in a library environment.

Problems Caused by Children in the Library

Noise
Even though most libraries have done away with the "Silent!" signs, we still need to keep the volume down so patrons can study. Over the last decade or two, most facilities have grown to tolerate more sound than in the past, but we still realize that we must continue to battle noise if we are to maintain an atmosphere conducive to reading.

(Continued)

Rambunctiousness

We want some activity, but running, jumping around, and lots of movement are just as disturbing as noise. People can't study with that kind of excess visual distraction.

Broken Rules

Sometimes they don't know all of the ins and outs of the library world, and other times it seems like they just don't care. They don't sign in to use the Internet computers, they don't go to the right place to check out books, six of them will sit at a table clearly designed for four, they expect to borrow pencils, and so on. Mostly it is just an extra hassle in maintaining the order we need to function, but it can be a significant burden, especially when we are often short-staffed.

Accidents

Little hands are busy but not always sure. Kids knock over books and displays, leave dirty fingerprints on tables, play on the computer keyboard until the computer makes a sound even Bill Gates has never heard, and generally have to touch and handle everything within reach. We childproof our children's areas as much as possible, but we can't anticipate and avoid every possible accident in the entire library.

Real Troublemaking

Kids in the library can lead to anything from mischievous pranks that can damage property to big problems like serious vandalism and destruction of property. Sometimes they are intrigued with such universal questions as how many paper towels can be stuffed into the toilet. Other times, the need to be a published author leads to "Jason was here" written on walls and books. It can be a need to show off one's computer expertise by leaving a nude photo on as the screensaver. Intentions can be worse, and so can the damage. It's always hard to catch a vandal in the library, and prosecuting them takes time and energy yet seldom undoes all the damage.

When we look at the problems we associate with children in the library, one fact should jump out at us. We can encounter these problems with any age group. We can certainly hear plenty of noise from a group of genealogists working on a project together. An active researcher can be back and forth, dragging books and magazines all over. The patrons may not move at the pace of a five-year-old, but they can still be just as distracting. No age group has a monopoly on avoiding, ignoring, or breaking rules. Accidents happen to everyone, and real problems in the library can be caused by patrons of any age. The library where I work suffered through two years of an individual actually defecating on certain books and leaving them in the men's room. When the police finally caught the individual, it turned out to be an engineer in his mid-fifties with top-secret clearance at the nearby military base. That's pretty serious vandalism, yet no teenager or child was involved. Granted, we are more likely to have a complaint about the preschool story time kids running all over the place than we are about the genealogists, but the important point is that we can encounter the same problems we face with kids from any age group.

Problems for Children in the Library

If the only challenge we face were getting kids to quiet down and walk, plus an occasional annoying case of vandalism, we wouldn't find the child issue so demanding. The sad fact is that this is like wading into the shark-infested water and worrying about getting your toes bit by a crab. There are other, much more serious problems to consider. They may come up less often, but that's only a small bit of comfort. Children at the library are unfortunately at risk for a number of dangers.

Injury
Libraries are mostly built with adult users in mind. Big and heavy doors, lots of people carrying armloads of books and unaware of anyone crawling near them, traffic whizzing past just outside the entry, and so forth all mean that serious injury is possible at any moment. Anyone who has ever been near a child when a accident has happened will say, "I just took my eye off her for a second."

Theft of Property
We are always telling people to watch their things. Kids are up and down constantly, leaving their possessions unattended, an easy target for a thief. Loss of a schoolbook or lunch money may not seem like the end of the world to us but can be extremely distressing to a child. It also colors their image of the library for a long time.

Fights
Kids get into fights. Watch any siblings and that fact becomes obvious. Sometimes, it is merely an irritation, but it can also be disruptive and dangerous. The real danger can come from kids picking on younger children or ganging up on one child. Because it is common for students to flow into the library directly from school, it has to be expected that the confrontations at school can flow into the library with them. (Continued)

Sexual Predators

Exhibitionists, molesters, and adults who prey on kids can all be found in public libraries. They can also be found in schools, alleys, churches, and the home. One of the most tragic truths to come to light in the last few years is exactly how often children are victimized. Because libraries are open and it is common for kids and adults to be in close proximity, it is a suitable spot for those who prey. We may not be at any greater risk than other public spots, but we are not at any less risk either.

Kidnapping

Lots of kids—and parents thinking the library staff are happy to watch them: what a great combination for a kidnapper. Kidnapping may be a part of a divorce fight as well as the act of a stranger. When we hear a child crying as an adult drags him or her out of the library, we can't be sure that it is the proper person taking the child.

It's painful to think about the reality that children are at risk in their public library, but we can't ignore it. We'd like to go back to the time when the library was a safe haven, but libraries aren't separate from what occurs in the larger society. That time in society when it was safe for children to play anyplace is gone (if it ever existed), and that time is also gone in libraries.

Just as we can't act in isolation from society in understanding the risks children face, we cannot separate ourselves from society, laws, and families in dealing with these risks. That's one of the greatest challenges in addressing kid issues. We can't just throw out a six-year-old troublemaker. Even an obnoxious fifteen-year-old gives us different issues than we would face with the same behavior in a twenty-two-year-old. We have to face some additional facts:

Parents have a role

This has always been the case, but it's more complex now. Years ago, in the time anthropologists refer to as the "Leave it to Beaver" era, the librarian could easily contact a parent and be reasonably assured that a proper attitude adjustment would result. Even the threat of contacting a parent was enough to bring most kids into line. Now it's difficult to even find the parents. It's even tough to know who the parent is in this day of divorce, blended families, and legal guardians. Even if the proper person can be contacted and notified, the odds of getting the response we want are low.

The parents often expect the library staff to handle their problems or even fail to recognize a problem. Even if the parents agree there is a problem, they can be too tired or too busy to effectively deal with the child's behavior at home, much less at the library. We even see more cases of the parents siding with their little angel, no matter what, and threatening to sue or otherwise teach us a lesson.

Laws are changing

Because society is changing, there is an effort to change our laws to recognize these new realities. That means laws are being passed to protect children and to spell out specific actions to address various situations. In some cases, such as notification laws, people who deal with children have legal obligations to report signs of child abuse. Agencies are being authorized to deal with problems that had always been strictly the jurisdiction of parents. Custodial laws give various rights to custodial and noncustodial parents. Library staff have not been directly mentioned in most of this barrage of new laws and regulations, but often they have to understand them to know what to do when a child is causing a problem. A simple phone call to mom isn't the only approach today.

Society is divided

We all want to support kids today, but society is strongly divided as to the best methods. There's a renewed interest in the "get tough" approach. Others feel kids need unconditional love. Self-esteem for kids is a popular topic with plenty of supporters and detractors. All of this societal attention means that our response to a specific problem can end up on the local news. We've seen it with schools frequently. A child is punished for taking medicine to school. A rowdy young child is put off the school bus two miles from home. These become local news items now, and the library is not immune from scrutiny. Although our institution enjoys generally better public approval than the schools, we live in a time when any place and anyone is open for public examination and even scorn. That means we have to remember that whatever we do, right or wrong, could end up on the front page of the local paper.

So we have to deal with rambunctious kids who may or may not be interested in our offerings, and can disturb the adult patrons who are; protect these same kids from accidents and the ugliest elements of our society; and do it in an environment of reduced parental support and increasingly confusing new laws. And you thought it would be a major challenge.

We have two choices:

1. Ban anyone under the age of twenty-one from the library.
2. Address the challenges of serving these little people with a comprehensive range of services, policies, training, and enforcement.

If you chose number 1, there's good news and bad news. The bad news is you will lose your funding and have to close your library. The good news is you can stop reading now.

Still here? That means you are willing to do the work necessary to develop a comprehensive approach to safely serving children in your library. Our program needs work toward achieving the following goals.

Goals

1. Protect children. They must be as safe as possible from risk of injury and harm from another person.
2. Protect children's right to use the library. In protecting them, we can't close off the reason they have for coming here.
3. Prevent them from interfering with other people's use of the library. We have to endure some disorder from their youthful enthusiasm, but we cannot let them significantly infringe on others' abilities to use the library in the manner it is intended. That may mean protecting children from the noise and distraction of other children.
4. Involve the outside world. Parents, teachers, legal guardians, grandparents, police, child protection agencies, and social service organizations are among the parties interested in how we deal with children. Sometimes, they can be part of the problem; frequently, they can be part of the solution.

The following guidelines illustrate the components of our plan to safely serve children in the library.

Guidelines

Apply the basic "Rules of Conduct" to children as well as adults
If our rules prohibit loud talking, we simply apply that rule to kids as well as grown-ups. Same with all the other rules. We should not tolerate more noise from youngsters because "they're just kids." Our reason for limiting

noise is to prevent disturbing other patrons, and we have to assume that noise that disturbs is unacceptable from either adults or children. That is also true with the other rules. We do have to make an exception for very young children crying and similar problems. We should only make these exceptions if a parent is present, and the parent should be addressing the child's behavior. If a child is crying and there is no one with the child, staff need to talk to the child and deal with the problem, both to reduce the noise problem and to provide any assistance the child needs. The key is to remember that the reason we have our rules in the first place is to help us provide a safe, pleasant environment where our patrons can use library services. Anything that interferes with this is a problem, whether the interference comes from a child or adult.

Develop and implement a special "Children in the Library" policy to deal with the unique issues presented by children

Our standard rules can't address everything we face in dealing with kids, so we do need to create a special set of policies to cover these areas. This is the document you will give parents if there are problems; it will advise staff how to handle such situations; and it will be the basis of staff training. This is not a document you normally need to post (just as most libraries don't post circulation policies), so it can be more detailed. Once it is adopted by the board of trustees, it gives staff some legal backing for any actions they need to take. That backing is always important but is even more crucial when dealing with minors. The policy needs to answer the following questions:

> What is the minimum age for a child to be in the library without a parent or guardian?
>
> What is the minimum age for the person supervising a child too young to be in the library alone? (Can a nine-year-old be in charge of a three-year-old?)
>
> How do staff handle children left at the library younger than this age?
>
> What happens to children left at the library at closing time? If there are different treatments for different ages, define the ages and the treatments.
>
> How are medical or other emergencies handled with children?
>
> How are rule violations handled for children if their parents are with them?
>
> How are rule violations handled for children without parents or guardians at the library?

Under what circumstances are children removed from the library?

When are they allowed back?

Are parents notified of their children's problems or removal? If so, how?

What organizations should be involved in handling problems (police, child protective services, etc.)?

Who contacts these groups and under what circumstances?

Are there other concerns related to children that need to be addressed?

A general opening statement expressing library philosophy can also be helpful. This could discuss the roles of the library, parents, and children; explain why the library felt a need to create this policy; emphasize the support of children in the library and the need to protect them; and so forth.

A "Children in the Library" policy needs to be developed with the input of all staff who work with children and any staff who deal with problems related to children, such as security guards. Like other policies, it needs to be reviewed and approved by legal counsel and the board. There should be copies freely available to hand out, especially when dealing with a problem.

If you want a "Children in the Library" policy to post, you can do a shorter "Rules for Children" document and note on this that the complete policy is available at the Children's Desk. Another option is a brief policy statement explaining a few key points, while the full procedures are spelled out in a separate document.That way you can display a readable document that deals with your major issues yet still have an official policy available. If you do this, the full policy can spell out all the details on consequences (e.g., what happens if children are left at closing time, etc.). Use your full policy as a handout when dealing with problems because you will want the parent to have a chance to read and understand all the issues libraries face with children.

Sample policies are available in appendix 3.

Train staff on the policy and how to apply it

The more specific your policy is, the easier it is to enforce. For example, your policy may state that "children over the age of fourteen who make too much noise or disturb other patrons will be given two warnings. After that, they will be told to leave the library. They may come back the next day. If they are removed from the library again that week, they will not be allowed back for thirty days. A letter explaining this thirty-day removal will be sent to the parent by the director." Here, everyone has a fairly good idea of the steps, actions, ages, and time lines. If your policy simply states that "children who violate library rules may be asked to leave the library," you either have to do detailed training or accept a wide variation on staff responses to problems. Training should deal with how to approach children, what to say to adults, and how to handle emergencies. Staff should be given specific examples of usable phrases. For example, a five-year-old child is unattended at the library and a staff member phones the parent: "Hello, my name is Mrs. Wilson. I'm the children's librarian at Dewey Public Library. Your son, Matthew, is here by himself. For the safety of the children, our policy requires that a parent or responsible adult accompany any child under the age of seven. Because Matthew is only five, we need you to have someone come to the library and either pick him up or stay with him. When can someone be here?"

If a child under the age of seven is running around the library and a parent is someplace in the library, introduce yourself to the child and explain that you work for the library. Ask who the child is here with. Walk around the library with the child to locate the adult. Introduce yourself to the adult, give him or her a copy of the policy, and say, "For the safety of children under the age of seven, our policy requires that parents be in direct supervision of their children. That means the parent should be able to see the child at all times. We are really concerned about the safety of children at the library."

If parents are unhappy about the need to keep an eye on their child, staff can use the comparison to a large shopping mall: "The library is no safer than the mall, and parents wouldn't leave a five-year-old out of their sight at the mall." Also be sure parents understand that library staff cannot watch the child. Explain that staff come and go to help patrons, conduct programs, go to lunch, and so forth. Parents need to know that the staff member who is in the children's room when the child comes in may be gone in a few minutes, replaced by someone who doesn't know if the child is leaving with a parent or a stranger. Parents may have quaint ideas about libraries, and staff need to clearly explain that they are not able to watch any child, even for a minute. It's better to disappoint a parent about the nature of libraries than to deal with them about a tragedy.

Training of staff in this area must be especially thorough. If there is ever an accident or other serious problem at the library, there can be a legal liability issue if policy was not followed.

Take the needed security precautions

Security is an issue for all patrons and staff, but because children are always the most vulnerable, special measures may be needed. The single most significant step is to enforce the rule against young children being left at the library. That means we must contact parents, police, or child services agencies every single time we think a young child is left unattended. These children are at the greatest risk, and we can never give in to the temptation to overlook it "just this one time." Staff diligence on this may be all there is to prevent a tragedy. Dealing with unattended children is time-consuming and diverts staff from routine job duties, but we just have to accept that as a fact of life and take each situation seriously. We would never choose to ignore a fire alarm, guessing that it is a mistake, and a young child left alone at the library can never be ignored either. If a specific child is being left regularly, involve the police and other authorities to put a stop to it, but never overlook a single child.

Security for children, like all security, involves alertness and observation of the situation. If an adult without a child is spending a great deal of time in the children's room, this needs attention. Although there are many legitimate reasons for this, there are also some criminal reasons. A library staff member should approach the adult, identify himself or herself, and ask if any help is needed. If the adult doesn't need help but continues to wander around the children's room, alert a guard (if you have one). Have a staff member around the adult, shelving books, straightening materials, and staying in sight. Sit at a study area and do some office work but be in the proximity. Observe and be visible. If you have reasons to believe the adult is following a child, talk to the person. This isn't easy because we don't want to suspect someone of being a child molester but neither can we let our reservations allow someone to endanger children. The best way to deal with this is to have two staff members ask to talk to the patron in an office. At least one should be a part of the senior administration. Explain that complaints have been received about him and staff have to follow up. He will probably be offended but explain that it is the library's obligation to do everything possible to protect children.

Let him know he has been observed in the children's room for X amount of time and did not seem to using any children's room materials. Ask why he is in there. If you don't get a satisfactory answer, it may be necessary to ask him to stay out of the room. Tell him that library staff will be happy to get any materials from the children's room he needs.

If you still have concerns about the person, contact the police. Ask them to come over so you can point the person out to them. It is possible the police may recognize him and can give some information.

This sounds like a big response to someone simply wandering around the children's room. It is. Not many adults will hang around this room without a reason, and usually it is clear what they are doing there. If not, then there is no other way to protect children at the library except to take active steps when someone is loitering around kids. Libraries are always popular places for people with nothing to do, but there is no reason we can't limit these people to the adult areas.

Another security step is to inspect your library, especially children's areas, for hidden corners. A big display may be attractive, but if it hides a section of the children's room, it needs a new location. Staff at the desks or their regular posts should have unobscured lines of sight throughout the children's room and as much of the library as possible. Rearrange furniture or add security mirrors if necessary. Be sure there are no dark areas and add lighting where needed inside and outside the building. Lighting is one of the best, most economical crime-prevention tools available. For libraries, it's especially handy because patrons want good light for reading anyway.

Stronger precautions may be considered, depending on your experience and level of concern. Many libraries lock their rest rooms or just the rest rooms near the children's area. Keys are available from staff. Rest rooms near the children's area can be limited to children and their parents, especially if the doors are locked. Post a simple sign stating this on the rest room door, and direct other patrons to the appropriate rest rooms.

An even more drastic step is to limit the children's room to kids under a certain age and their family members. You may need to make some sort of exception for adults studying children's literature and adults working with kids, such as teachers, day-care staff, and so forth. This is a difficult to enforce rule (i.e., what is proof of parenthood, anyway?) and will likely lead to staff having to deal with confused, unhappy patrons. The "safety of children" explanation goes a long way, but it doesn't guarantee every patron's happiness or compliance. Before posting a rule such as this, check with your library's legal authority to see if there are any problems with this approach. It is a good way to protect children but will cause significant staff effort, especially at first. Note that it also does not protect children in other parts of the library.

A new concern is the young age of some people who assault children. Kids in their early teens and even younger have committed sex crimes and other crimes against young children. Although we are keeping the "weird-looking old man" out of the children's room, we unfortunately can't forget that children are hurting children. It's a confusing world, but we have to accept reality. Again, ensuring that parents are with their young children is our best approach. Being alert and responding to a child who seems scared or upset are also important. We can't ignore a child just because we don't see any ominous-looking people around.

Involve the community

We can't do everything ourselves. There is help available. If you are having any problems with unattended children, invite someone from the child services agencies to meet with staff. Discuss the issues and find out what services are offered. Know how to contact the appropriate agency before it's an emergency. It's always helpful to develop a working relationship with a couple of individuals at each agency. It's easier to call and ask for a specific person. He or she may even be willing to help with staff training. It shouldn't be a one-way street. Explore how the library can help them. Usually these agencies need help getting the word out about their services and issues.

Posting fliers, putting up an informative display mixing their materials with library books, and creating bibliographies and book marks can help you and them. Other organizations may also be interested.

Every library seeks to provide a stimulating yet safe and controlled environment for our young users. We need to allow them to be kids—lively, curious, challenging—although at the same time we need to ensure that they do not prevent other patrons from doing their library work. It will always be a tall order to protect these little people and at the same time protect the library from them. To do this means being alert and a little protective, developing policies that support our efforts, and training the staff to follow through. Parents and outside organizations offer significant assistance.

Frankly, it is a lot of effort to accomplish all this. It is worth it, however. These kids running through the stacks today will be running the country in a few years. We have to help them grow into that task. We also must remember that they are the ones who will be responsible for putting us in nursing homes, so we better be kind to them!

13

Censorship Problems

The last several years have seen a steady increase in attempts to remove material from libraries. Something about a request to remove a book hits most of us hard and emotionally. It's like a slap in the face, and we often take it that way. Even if we don't verbalize our feelings, our body language and attitude often reveal our feelings. We feel attacked, adopt a defensive state of mind, and feel a need to protect the principles of libraries. A simple request from a patron, no matter how polite, is a conflict situation. They want us to take something out that we decided the public should have available. They are trying to rob the public of views, and we will defend the right to read. If that's the case with a polite request, imagine the feelings when a customer rudely demands a removal.

The additional complication that separates censorship conflicts from most difficult patron issues is that they can lead to all sorts of media coverage. And, in some situations, there is the possibility that a sizable portion of the public may agree with the patron, something that is unlikely to happen when we are dealing with a drunk in the library.

This high-profile, highly emotional issue can be handled professionally by setting goals and by following guidelines.

Goals

1. Treat the patron and the request with respect and courtesy.
2. Be sure that the patron knows you will use your established procedure to give the request serious consideration. Make sure the patron knows the library's review process and any appeal avenues.
3. The patron should feel you are working with him or her to solve a joint problem.
4. Be able to demonstrate to any open-minded outside person that the library has been fair and reasonable.

The first step in controlling the situation with a censorship request is to try to understand the person making the request. The fact that someone requests that material be removed from a collection does not mean he or she is set on creating problems. Most people who request that we remove something from the library do not think of themselves as censors. They see their actions as removing a danger from the community. Most will even state, "I don't like censorship, but this book. . . ." To them, it is like cleaning up broken glass in the road in front of their homes—it's a neighborly act. In many cases, these patrons are actually loyal library users and often supporters. They usually understand the concept of providing access to a variety of views but have found a book or video that goes too far for them. They can take some differences of opinions but not too much.

Sometimes, a patron will simply return a book and mutter, "I can't believe that the library uses tax money to buy this kind of filth," and walk off. Other times, a patron will come to the desk, often with book or video in hand, and ask, "Do you know what this book is about? You need to get this out of the library," and wait for your response. In either case, our response can make for a smooth or difficult interaction. However, if we as library staff handle the initial inquiry and request poorly, it can make a sometimes difficult situation much worse.

Here are some tips for successful interactions:

Guidelines

Give the patron your full attention

Listen to all comments, whether the person wishes to make a formal complaint or not. Often, those who make a complaint expect a hostile reaction from library staff. Because of this, it's even more important that we proceed in a positive manner, so both the library and the patron can focus on the issue of the material and not create anything that could be perceived as a power struggle or a personal confrontation. It's important not just that we listen, but that we demonstrate that *we are* listening. Don't discharge books or stamp due-date cards when the patron is talking about the book. You may be able to accomplish simple tasks such as this while giving full attention to the comments, but the patron does not know this. If the patron talks to a friend about the process of making a complaint, we don't want it said that "the librarian just kept on stamping cards and didn't even pay attention to what I said."

Avoid labels and loaded words

Even if we consider the person a *censor*, never use that term to him or her. Such patrons are exercising their rights and shouldn't be labeled just because we are inconvenienced or disagree with it.

Don't get into arguments on controversial topics

If the complaint, for example, concerns a book about homosexuality, you will never win a debate on the topic. People may ask, "Would you want your kids reading this?" or "You don't think it's okay for two men to live together and raise a child, do you?" Personal views on these issues are not relevant to these discussions and should never be expressed. Our role at the library is to offer a wide variety of topics to meet the needs of the public, and that's your only opinion.

Explain the materials-selection policy

If the person wants to hear why you have such a book or video, explain your policy for choosing books or videos, the obligation to meet the needs of a wide audience, and so forth. Everyone on staff should know the policy, how to handle complaints, and what to do if a patron wants to file a formal request for reconsideration. Even if your library's policy is to have complaints handled by a supervisor, everyone who has any dealing with the public must know how to reply to a complaint on material. Have a copy of the policy available to distribute. If you don't provide a copy, it will look like your library is conducting business in secret, raising suspicions. The materials-selection policy should spell out clearly what steps the patron needs to take to formally request material be removed, including what happens after the request is submitted, who will respond, and time lines. Be open about the library's procedures for choosing and reviewing materials.

Any request for reconsideration is public record

Reconsideration requests can be read by media or any other interested party. If the complaint becomes a media issue, it's awkward if library staff are asked to explain why the material is being challenged. We don't want to say negative things like "it will corrupt children," and paraphrasing the complainant is tricky. We can be accurate by showing the actual written complaint. The form should state that it is public record and available.

Work with patrons as much as possible

Offer to add materials with their point of view, help with lists of what you have on all sides of the topic, and so forth. This approach will show a willingness to be fair, which may help if the material is not removed. Additionally, if this ever becomes a public feud, it's important that the library can prove it has been as reasonable and accommodating as possible. We may not change the minds of the people who file the complaint, but we will show those who are impartial that we handled the issue fairly.

If we listen and respect others' opinions and views, there will not be too many instances where the person wishing to remove material will become a problem patron.

Situation of the Day

A visibly upset mother approaches the circulation desk with a book in her hand:

"I just got this book, *Daddy's Roommate*, off the children's shelf. Look at these pictures—two men in bed with each other! Little children shouldn't be able to see this sort of thing. How can I try to give my kids good values when they can come in here and see this? I thought the library was supposed to be a wholesome place for families."

How do you respond?

"We have books like *Daddy's Roommate* because teachers and parents have requested information on this topic. We do have lots of books that show traditional family values. I can help you find some of those if you'd like," says the library staffer.

"What about kids who see this, though? It's going to confuse them. Books like this teach that homosexuality is normal," the patron responds.

"Our library has thousands of users, and we have to have a wide selection to meet everyone's needs. Some people need books like this. If, for example, a teacher has a child in her class who lives with two fathers, the teacher can use a book like this to deal with questions. The library doesn't say what's right or wrong, but we have to have a wide range to reflect today's society."

"I don't think you should have anything like this. Kids can never learn what's right or wrong today if we keep showing them all these things."

"Well, there are a few things I can do. If you want, I can get our director to talk to you about this more. Or, if you want, there is a process to request that a book be removed from the library system. Let me give you a copy of our "Materials-Selection Policy." It explains how we decide which books we buy, and here is information about how you can request that we remove a book."

Keys to Success

At no point does the library staff member discuss her views on homosexuality, children, today's society, or other hot topics.

It's not necessary to respond to every single comment, such as "Libraries should be wholesome places" or "How can I show my kids what's right and wrong?" Keep the focus on the library's role of providing information to the entire community.

Have the "Materials-Selection Policy" handy and offer that option without making the patron suggest it. A good policy will spend a little time discussing the library's goal of providing information for all and the philosophy of choosing material to reflect today's society.

The staff member realized when the discussion had gone as far as she could take it. She politely explained the library's reasoning but resisted the temptation to get into an extended argument that she could not win. After explaining, she gave the patron options about how she could pursue this if she wished. It was up to the patron to either talk to the director (or other appropriate management person) or look into filing a formal complaint.

14

A Brief History of Communication

All the communication theory you need in five minutes.

In the opening of Stephen Hawkings' *A Brief History of Time*, he wrote about being told that for every equation he put in his book he would lose 10,000 sales. He only included one formula: $e=mc^2$. He decided that it was worth losing all those sales because this one equation was so important.

I think it's a little like that for library training manuals. Library staff want practical information, not a lot of theory. I had planned to keep all the theory out of this, but I am weak and had to include just a bit. There is real value in learning how communication works. All human interactions operate on basically the same foundation. Once you understand the simple theory behind communication, you will find ways to improve your own skills. You'll see others and learn from their mistakes and pick up on their strengths. Even in unfamiliar, unexpected circumstances, you will have solid footing. So, at the risk of losing 10,000 sales, here's the process:

Susan walks up to the circulation desk. She thinks to herself, "I want that person behind the desk to get the book I have on reserve." For her to actually make this statement, she encodes the message into words and transmits the words along with body language, facial expression, voice tone, and possibly other visual aides. In this case, Susan has the reserve notice in her hand, so she places it on the circulation desk in front of our librarian, Gwen. When sending her request, Susan includes any emotions she is feeling. She may be happy about getting the book, worried about missing her next appointment, or suffering from a toothache. This emotional content, related to the message or not, is woven into her words and even more into her tone and body language.

Gwen, hearing the request, decodes the words and nonverbal actions to arrive at her understanding of Susan's request. Unconsciously, she is adding context to Susan's message, such factors as the time of day and visual information about how Susan is dressed, the way she placed the reserve note on the desk, and so forth. Gwen is also now adding information to the request about her knowledge of how reserves are handled.

Both *sender* and *receiver* code and decode messages to include their existing perceptions, biases, language ability, emotional state, social status, and other internal factors. External factors, constantly changing, are also plugged into this equation.

This extremely simple example illustrates how many factors go into each snippet of dialogue we have. The important point is that even in this routine conversation, there are endless variables that can cause even the most basic conversation to go astray. Susan could have been fidgeting, knowing she had only two minutes until the bus arrived outside. Gwen could interpret the fidgeting as a commentary on the time it is taking to handle this request and get annoyed. "What does she want?! I'm going as fast as I can!" she may think, never realizing the fidgeting had nothing to do with her at all.

That type of confusion is common. Most of the message sent or received have nothing to do with the library. Here are a couple examples:

> A homeless-looking person approaches the desk and says meekly, "Excuse me, could you help me, please?" If the person behind the desk has worked in urban areas for a long time, he may suspect that this is not a library question but a come-on for money. Based on this suspicion, he may respond sternly or not at all. Someone new, who has never been approached for money, will walk over expecting some kind of library question. Two people seeing the exact same person, reading the exact same gestures, and hearing the exact same words will interpret the situation in completely different ways. They will also formulate their responses and encode their messages differently, based on how they decoded this simple comment.

In an Internet class, the instructor gave this simple command: "Use this mouse to point and click." One student picked up the mouse, aimed it at the screen, and clicked, like using a remote control for a TV. I saw this happen, and it does not mean that the person is stupid. The receiver simply translated the sender's words using the only frame of reference available. Other students may have used the mouse to point and click in previous computer applications so they could make a more appropriate interpretation of the instruction.

These examples illustrate one of the keys in communication: the listener determines what message is communicated. No matter what is said or how it is said, ultimately it is the way the listener interprets the signals that decides what is communicated. Slang gives us more examples. If a teenager says that a movie is "bad," his friends will want to see it, but older folks would have considered that a negative review. Both heard the same word but interpreted it differently. What does this mean, other than we shouldn't let teenagers do movie reviews? It means that you, as the listener, have the key role in making communication work. Your ability to interpret will decide how smoothly the communication will go.

Because of this, our listening skills are crucial. We are responsible for paying careful attention to the speaker and accurately interpreting the words and body language so we grasp the message.

Key Point

Understanding the role of the listener can help us send our messages more accurately. Because the listener is determining what is communicated, we must do all we can to ensure that the message received is the message we want sent. When speaking, one of our goals should be to help others be better listeners. We can do this by speaking and sending our message in the most appropriate manner for that listener. As speakers, we should think about the listener's frame of reference and tailor our message to him or her. That's really the key to becoming a successful communicator.

For example, if I am going to explain to a businessperson why we don't allow reference books to go out, I may talk about our budget: we can't afford to buy many copies, and our bottom line need is to keep some expensive books available at all times. If I am going to answer that same question from a fifth-grader, I will talk about all the other fifth-graders who have to use this book to get their homework done and the library can only work if we all share and take turns. The same message is given—we need the book to be available for others—but it is encoded differently to give each listener the best chance of decoding it in a way that is similar to what I wanted to him or her to hear. We can use the fact that all listeners decode using their own biases, perceptions, and so forth to our advantage. We simply send a message that fits within their frame of reference.

Before sending any significant message, ask yourself these two vital questions:

1. What is my message?

2. Who is my audience?

Don't speak until you can answer those questions. Know what you want to say and how to say it to best be understood by your listener. This works whether you are training your dog, apologizing to your spouse, or calming down an upset patron.

And that's all the communication theory you need to know. It isn't rocket science.

15

Listening Takes
More than Ears

*You have two ears and one mouth because God wants you
to listen twice as much as you talk.*

—My mother (and possibly every other mother in history)

Listening Is a Skill

Listening is a popular topic today, and there's a good reason for that. People are beginning to realize one simple truth: listening, not talking, is the key to communication.

Listening is a skill. It has to be learned and practiced, just like any other skill. Unfortunately, it's seldom taught in school. We had to give talks in class to learn how to speak, but what did we do to learn how to listen?

Not only is listening seldom taught, but it isn't even demonstrated often in life. Have you ever had this experience? You have major news you have to tell someone. You come up to a friend and say, "My wife just ran off with my best friend. My life is ruined!" only to have your friend reply, "That's a bummer. Can you give me a ride to the shop? They called and said my car's ready."

That kind of response makes you doubt that you really have a friend. He was too focused on his own issue to listen to you. When something is important to you, you want the person you are conversing with to acknowledge that your message was heard and understood. You don't expect them to fix the problem, just to let you express your views on it. This is called *empathetic listening*, and it can make a world of difference, in the library or in any other circumstance.

Because it is so rare to find a really good listener, many people don't know how significant it can be. To have another human being truly listen, truly understand your thoughts and fears, is a powerful experience. It opens the door to a deeper level of connection than we experience in ordinary life, where we are accustomed to people walking the opposite direction and asking, "How are you?" Typically, they don't want more than the standard one-word response: "Fine." When we find someone who asks, "How are you?" and stops to listen for a real answer, we are pleasantly surprised. We feel a little more connected to that person and a little less isolated from the world.

So what does this have to do with libraries and dealing with difficult people? Everything! Lack of listening skills can lead to problems and make any problem we encounter worse. Good listening skills can prevent many problems as well as solve some we come across. Listening to and understanding the other person open the door to effective communication, in the library and in the rest of the world.

Situation of the Day

A depressed, middle-aged woman called a suicide prevention center hotline.

"My problem is family. I think they hate me and wish I was dead. Even my husband ignores me. This has been going on so long that I feel alone all the time. It's made me really depressed."

"It sounds like you are depressed and lonely because your family and husband ignore you. Is that right?" asked the volunteer on the other end of the phone.

"That's exactly it," said the caller, with a trace of excitement in her voice.

"That must be really hard for you. Can you tell me a little about what has happened to make you feel this way?" asks the volunteer.

The call proceeds, with the caller telling of incidents and feelings and the volunteer never saying more than "Tell me more about . . . ," "How does that make you feel?" and "Go on."

After talking for about 45 minutes, the caller is running out of steam. "Thank you for all your help. I feel a lot better," she says.

The volunteer did not offer one word of advice, didn't recommend a self-help book or new therapy, and didn't perform any counseling. The volunteer simply listened. He let her talk without making any judgments, telling her what to do, or offering such platitudes as "Don't worry. It will get better." As the conversation proceeded, the caller gained faith in the volunteer and realized she could say what she felt without fear of criticism. Some people have never really been listened to, and the feeling is freeing. Simply talking with a good listener lifts some of the burden.

Now, just think—if this listening skill can make a big difference in a life-or-death situation, it must be useful in dealing with our library challenges. We know that we must make the patron feel respected or he will feel slighted and work to gain control. His efforts may include yelling or other undesirable behaviors. Listening carefully is one of the best ways to make a person feel respected. It creates a connection, and the patron can feel that you are working with him to solve a common problem, rather than fighting him. It also helps you get an accurate idea of what the patron needs and how you can help. Listening is one of the keys to preventing problems at the library.

Myths about Listening

Are you a good listener? One way to find out is to see how much you know about this skill.

Myth 1
If someone is quiet while
you are talking, they are listening.

How often have you made a to-do list for the afternoon, planned your weekend, or just took a mental nap while someone was talking to you? You might as well admit it; we've all done it from time to time. That means the next time you are trying hard to make a point and the person you are talking to is just sitting there, you know you can't assume that he or she is really listening to you. Sometimes the person is just waiting for his or her turn to talk. It's not a dialogue; it's two monologues.

Myth 2
Hearing is the same as listening.

Hearing is what our ears do. *Listening* is what our mind does. That's a huge difference. I can hear someone speak in Greek to me, but it's hard for me to really listen because I don't speak Greek. I can't understand the words, and I can't get the message. Listening means interpreting the words to get a message. It also means observing facial expressions and body language plus considering the context of the situation. Adding all these clues together is part of listening.

Myth 3
Listening is a passive skill.

Listening requires a great deal of effort. That's especially true with a difficult person or in a tense situation. You exert effort to block out distractions. You work to get the real meaning from the words. You try hard to add the body language to the words to get the entire message. Nothing passive about it.

Myth 4
You can stop listening once
you get the gist of the message.

That means you are making the assumption that you know what point the speaker is going to make. And we know the dangers of assumptions. One time our library had just completed a long, public battle over *Daddy's Roommate* and related titles. We had been the target of an organized effort to remove these books, and I had heard lots of complaints, some in a less-than-kind manner. The issue was front page news and the number-one story on TV, especially when our board of trustees voted to keep the books at a contentious public meeting.

I was happy with the results but still a little battle weary a few days later when a young mother approached me and asked, "Do you have those books with two men in bed together?" "Yes," I said, trying to gather the energy to go through one more explanation. "Are they still in the children's room?" she asked. "Yes," I said, getting ready to launch into my speech about why we had them, why they are located in the children's room, what the board voted, and so forth. Before I could start, she said, "Good. I really need that book for my son in first grade. I'm glad you kept them," and off she went. If I had jumped in when I wanted to with my oh-so-eloquent defense, before she got to the gist of her questions, I would have at the least made a fool of myself. Because of the negativity in recent days and all the complaints I personally had to listen to, my assumptions were way off. One conversation that started like this one ended up with the patron informing me of the warm climate I was destined for in the afterlife. I assumed this was going to go that same way. It was luck, not skill, that kept me from going with those assumptions, but I did learn a useful lesson. Listen to the entire message before reacting.

Myth 5
Some people are born
good listeners and others aren't.

Great baseball players will tell you of childhoods spent swinging the bat hundreds of times every day, practicing instead of running around with the other kids, and constantly working to build their skills. By the time such an athlete is in his early twenties and stardom is predicted, announcers start heaping praise on this "natural, gifted athlete." His gift, more than athletic ability, was the determination to build his natural skills as much as possible.

Listening is a skill also, and it can be developed. Developing this skill means sacrificing your turn to talk so you can ask a follow-up question to the speaker. It means learning how to be silent for a few moments to give the speaker a chance to express some other important thought. Conscious effort and repeated attempts are required to develop this skill. Then you can smile to yourself when a friend says, "You're a natural listener."

Barriers to Listening

Why do many people have trouble listening? There are obstacles to overcome, and many of them come into play at the library. There are specific techniques, fortunately, to help us overcome these barriers. Let's start by identifying what we have to overcome.

Internal Distractions

There are so many ways we can zone out that this is the biggest barrier to listening. Worrying about whether your replacement at the desk will be late again, wondering when can you call home to see if the kids are still fighting, cursing your aching head, calculating the number of days until payday compared to the number of days until the bills need to be paid are all internal distractions. We sometimes add to the symphony by doing several things at once—stamping due-date cards, discharging books, and more. Inside your head there can be so much activity that there is no room for something new that demands all your attention, like an upset patron. Internal distractions are an example of that old saying, "It's all in your head." Unfortunately, that's where listening occurs also.

Physical Distractions

The copy machine, a crying child, printers, a loud truck rumbling by, a boisterous conversation a few feet away—all these common sounds can be significant barriers. They can lead to missed words and misunderstanding and cause the speaker to raise his or her voice to be heard. Unfortunately, this can easily be misinterpreted as yelling in anger. Physical distractions can also break your concentration. For example, if you are talking to a patron and a friend walks by and waves, it's likely you will miss a bit of the patron's message. Maybe it's not enough to do any damage to the overall communication, but if it happens several times it can be a real issue.

Emotional Distractions

It's hard to listen attentively if you are nervous, intimidated, or otherwise distracted emotionally. If a patron is yelling and scaring you, it's much more difficult to grasp the meaning of his or her words. You may understand the emotional message, but that's all. If you are having a hard time with a pushy patron and you know your supervisor is standing nearby and can observe the entire situation, you may think more about how this will show up on next week's evaluation than what the patron is actually saying. An extra complication here is that some people actually try to rattle you. They feel they get some sort of advantage by intimidating the person they see as their opponent in a discussion. It can work too, because we want to get the heck out of the situation and will bend any rule we can just to get such mean jerks out of our lives.

Defensive Listening

Do you ever start a debate in your mind with a speaker you disagree with? That's common, but the result is we are not listening as effectively once we start debating. We are not hearing as much because we are not paying full attention. Even more significantly, we are not open to the full range of the speaker's possible meanings. We have already made decisions about what is being said and about the speaker. After that, it's natural to try to make anything else said fit our judgments, no matter what the speaker means. We will put our spin on every word and nuance so everything falls neatly into our preset notions.

Perception

Be honest with yourself—do you take into account the appearance of the speaker when listening? Most of us do, even if we believe we shouldn't. When we are approached by a patron dressed nicely in a suit and tie, making his request in a firm but polite manner, we are likely to listen more carefully to him than to the homeless bag lady. The perception barrier can really come into play when we are talking with someone we know but don't like or respect. A coworker you consider to be rude and unprofessional comes up to you and says, "You didn't handle that last lady very well." You probably won't take that comment to heart as you might if the same words were spoken by a coworker you consider to be one of the best in your library and someone you personally like.

Misunderstandings

It can be a language barrier or a physical speech difficulty, for example, but we can easily tune out someone we have trouble hearing. A language barrier can include jargon, which we can easily lapse into. Have you ever watched people listening to a real computer geek talking to noncomputer people? When he's speaking in full geek mode, the noncomputer folks will zone out quickly because they can't understand a word of his language. We can do the same in the library world. Talking about claims returned, system overrides, or cataloging issues can quickly make a listener tune out. Even if the person does stay with us, there's a good chance he or she won't really understand what we tried to communicate. We both end up frustrated, and that is an easy situation for emotional responses.

Too Much Information

Another cause of tuning out is *information overload*. There's only so much we can think about at a time before we decide "enough already." At that point our brain takes us on a pleasant vacation to the beach while the speaker babbles ever onward. This can easily happen when we are trying to communicate to a patron. We have our points we want to make, in a well-intentioned effort to explain why the library policy exists, but we can overwhelm a patron. Then nothing gets heard. The more emotional the situation, especially the state of the listener, the lower the tolerance for new information.

Removing the Barriers

Learn to Listen

Barriers can be internal or external, and often we are dealing with a combination. If we know what the barriers are, we can look for opportunities to tear them down. Let's look at some useful tools to improve our ability to listen and accurately understand what others are saying.

Choose to listen

This may sound silly at first, but many people are not good listeners because they don't want to be. They either don't care, don't see the value, or don't make the effort. One of the first and simplest steps we can take to improve our listening habits is to decide to be a better listener. Make it a priority to pay attention and learn what the speaker is truly trying to communicate. At the core of this is a decision to value the other person more than we had. To listen attentively, we have to make our own concerns and wants secondary to the speaker's.

Focus completely on the speaker

Remember that listening is an active skill, not a passive one. Clear out all other distractions and pay complete attention. We can't treat the speaker like Muzak in the grocery store and still expect to get the correct message.

Remove physical distractions

Look for loud printers, copy machines, or other noisy machines that are too near places where there are frequent patron conversations. You wouldn't want the copier in your meeting room because of the noise and distractions. That same argument should lead us to move these noisy machines as far as we can from any service desks. For security reasons, we usually don't want these machines hidden; but we can design good line-of-sight floor plans where we can see them but not be blasted by the sound. To paraphrase an old saying about children, "Office machines should be seen and not heard." Sometimes, removing physical distractions means walking with the patron to a slightly less distracting location to complete the conversation. It could be a meeting room or a table in the public study area. Remember, security considerations, such as alerting a coworker that your are leaving, are important when deciding where to have a meeting with a patron, especially an upset individual.

Make eye contact

Much of any message is nonverbal, and you can't pick up nonverbal cues without looking at the speaker. A person's facial expression adds meaning and context to the words. This is especially important because words and phrases can have more than one meaning, and we need help to choose the correct meaning. Facial expressions and body language give us some of that help. Looking away means missing half the message. It's like reading a book with every other word crossed out.

Take notes

This is especially helpful with long, rambling conversations where it can be difficult to catch the main point. Your notes should be very brief, just a few words or phrases on the main point. Trying to write everything down becomes a distraction in itself.

Ask clarifying questions

"Tell me what you mean by. . . ." "Now, exactly when did you first report this. . . ." It's a good idea to start asking these questions before you get too lost. Give the speaker time to make a point, but don't let the conversation go too far before asking clarifying questions. Once you're lost, it requires more effort to get back on track.

Offer summarizing statements

"So, you've told us that you never had this book checked out, and you are still getting overdue notices. Is that correct?" "Let me be sure I understand. You want to renew this book for your mother, who is in the hospital, and you don't have her card, right?" Summarizing statements are best used after listening for awhile and checking to see that you properly interpreted the message before taking any action. Your voice tone is important here. Sometimes, when we have listened to someone ramble it's easy to sound a little frustrated when summarizing. We can also sound incredulous if the request seems off the wall. "You really are asking to check out a *reference book*; is that it?" Remember, as we are picking up their nonverbals, they are picking up ours, so our summarizing statements must be worded and expressed in a non-judgmental manner.

Silence
Giving the speaker opportunity to gather his or her thoughts can really help. Just as we may have trouble speaking if we feel rushed, others may have this trouble, too. Five seconds of silence seem like a long time, but if we can get used to it, we will give the speaker a valuable extra opportunity to complete his or her thoughts.

Observe body language to check your understanding
If you think the conversation is wrapping up, for example, check to see if the person is giving the same signs. Is he or she putting things away, smiling, nodding, looking at her watch, or saying "Thank you?" Or is the patron still standing there, looking confused or unsure? If you see any signs at all that what you think you heard disagrees with the body language, stop and check things out. Ask clarifying questions, such as "Did this completely answer your question?" or "Is there something else I can do to help?"

Keep an open mind
Our perceptions shape how we listen, and these perceptions can lead to receiving the wrong message. We all have biases. Although we think of them as regarding race, gender, national origin, and so forth, our biases can also be triggered by a person's clothing, use of language, social status, physical appearance, or age. The first step in dealing with our own biases is recognizing them. Hold any judgments, perceptions, and assumptions until you have all the information you need. Then, make only those judgments you absolutely need to make to address the library issue at hand. We don't need to decide if this is a good or bad person to handle most questions.

Span the gap
There is also a sort of biological imbalance that makes listening a challenge. We speak at about 100 to 150 words per minute. Our brains, however, can process 400 to 800 words per minute. That gap gives us plenty of

time to pay minimal attention to the speaker and still daydream for 40 seconds out of every minute. It's like a little paid vacation. However, it's also a trap because these internal distractions can lead us too far from the conversation. We might think we can wander away from the station for just a little bit, but that may be long enough to miss the train.

We need to turn this gap into an advantage we can use to improve our communicating. This extra time can be used to pay more attention to body language and see if it agrees with your understanding of the message. Take a few brief notes. Think about any clarifying questions you may need to ask. Decide if there is someone available with more expertise on the matter you can contact. Basically use any extra "processing power" your brain has to augment the communication, not escape it.

Learn to Communicate

Now that you know a little more about improving your listening skills, you can help others to be better listeners and you can also improve your communication with them.

Here are some practical ways you can help others to be better listeners and improve your chances of being understood.

Get to the point quickly

We know that people may lose their concentration quickly and start daydreaming. It's to everyone's advantage if we reduce the chance for that by stating our case in the most succinct way possible. If you have several points to make, break them down and discuss each one separately. We know it's easy for a listener to get confused about the speaker's main point, so make it easy by just making one point at a time and wrapping that up before going on to the next item. It's the same logic that allows meetings to go much smoother if everyone has an agenda and follows it.

Avoid jargon

Speaking plainly is always good, but it is even more important when you are the "expert." Believe it or not, that's how you are perceived when you are behind the desk—whether it's the circulation desk or a reference desk. The patron does not know if this is your first week on the job or the last day of a thirty-year career. To patrons, you are the one behind the desk, so you are the expert. If we talk about system overrides, cataloging protocols, or other technical topics, we can expect our listeners to zone out.

Be sure your listener is staying with you

The same way you can use clarifying questions or summarizing statements to be sure you understand, you can use them to be sure you are understood. Ask "Are you familiar with our new policy for circulating videos?" before you go into a discussion based on the assumption that the patron knows this policy. This helps to avoid information overload and removes a good excuse for the listener to zone out.

Use visual aids

If you are explaining a policy, for example, give the patron a copy of the policy to follow along. People process information in different ways. Some learn best by seeing, others by hearing. If you give a copy of the policy while you talk about it, you've doubled your chances of being heard and understood.

Speak in a positive, nonconfrontational manner

We know that emotions make it harder to hear and understand. We want to put our listener at ease so he or she can focus on what we are saying and not be distracted by nervousness, anger, or other emotions. Remember, that position behind the desk makes you an authority figure as well as an expert. You have the power to waive fines, reserve books, and look up all types of top-secret information in that computer you control. It may not seem like much to you but think about the patron's viewpoint. She has fines on a book she doesn't think she ever took out and now needs to get another book. You can grant her or deny her that book, so that is power. If we put our discussion in a positive tone so the patron feels like we are teaming with her to solve this problem, it's likely that she won't be distracted from listening due to emotions.

Most of us will go to great efforts to make ourselves heard. Do we go to the same efforts to hear others? Making the effort and using these techniques will help you through the toughest situation, in the library or out.

Listening Exercises

Now it's time to get out there and listen. Test one or two of the methods to improve your listening skills and see what results you get. Here are a few possibilities:

At the next meeting you attend, resolve that you will ask at least two clarifying questions.

The next time you talk with a friend about something your friend thinks is serious, focus all your attention on the speaker's issue. Ask him to tell you more about something that is important to him. Don't bring in any of your news or comments until you are sure he has completely finished.

Watch a silent movie or turn off the sound on a talkie and pay attention to how messages are communicated without words. How did the actors move to express shock, outrage, fear, love, or joy without any words? Watch facial expressions, gestures, posture, and body movement.

Pay attention to conversations between other people. Do they seem to be good listeners? Why? Can you see times when someone was interrupted or misunderstood? What facial expressions tipped you off? If you watch, you can often see when the speaker and listener were on two different wavelengths. See if you can tell when the conversation went off course.

Watch a conversation in a restaurant, bar, or airport where you can see people but not hear them. See how much of the conversation you can follow. What emotions are being expressed?

16

Your Communication Toolbox

SCARECROW:	I haven't got a brain . . . only straw.
DOROTHY:	How can you talk if you haven't got a brain?
SCARECROW:	I don't know . . . But some people without brains do an awful lot of talking . . . don't they?

— The Wizard of Oz

The scarecrow was right, as always. Brains are not required for talking. They do come in handy for communicating, however. That's important at the library because good communication skills are at the heart of preventing problems and handling difficult situations when they do arise.

Each of us has our own unique style of communicating. We have some instances when we shine and some when we are a little less gleaming. Over the years, you've probably learned a few things to say or do that help out in tough situations. It could be an icy stare that stops unwanted inquiries or a funny saying from your father that eases tensions; or maybe you just walk away from offensive conversations. These things are part of your style and resources you can draw on when needed.

If you find enough of these successful techniques, you will have a repertoire of tricks you can use to handle communication challenges. Think of it as your toolbox—the right tool for the right situation. Assembled here are some tried-and-true communication skill builders to add to your toolbox. Take a look and see if there are any you can use the next time you face a flat on the highway of life.

Use "I" statements

One of the keys to communication is making a connection between the speaker and listener. Once that bridge is built, understanding is increased and the exchange goes smoother. An "I" statement is an easy, effective way to build that bridge. When we speak to a patron on behalf of the library, we use such terms as "The library," "Our rules," and "We have a policy." Sometimes this is appropriate, but other times we can make more progress by personalizing the conversation. For example, if we can't help a patron, saying "I'm sorry" is better than "sorry." Saying, "I'll try to help you with this" connects you with the patron, shows concern, and breaks down institutional barriers.

Build empathy by showing you care

Empathy is an awareness of and concern for the other person's feelings. It may not be the same as *understanding* because we can't always feel what another is going through. Empathy, however, is a demonstrable effort to understand as much as possible. It's a way to connect at an emotional level, which can be necessary when dealing with an emotional person. There's a simple technique to show empathic feelings. You simply reflect the person's feelings back to them. For example, let's say you have to tell a homeless person to stop asking other patrons for money, and he responds by becoming agitated, saying this rule is unfair. You want to explain the reason for the rule, but he will listen better to you if you first connect with him. "I know you're unhappy about this rule. I can tell it's a problem for you." Reflecting works in conjunction with "I" statements to make people feel that others listen to them and respect their feelings. It's good to allow some silence after a reflecting statement. The person may want to respond with a little more, or he may be ready to listen to your next comments. Give him a chance to vent a little more before going into an explanation of the rule and other ways you can address his issues.

Remember that it is common for people to fight to be heard, and if we seem to ignore someone, it becomes more likely that he or she will make an effort to gain our attention. Such efforts include yelling or other unwanted behaviors. Once we have convinced the patron that we are listening and understanding his or her feelings, the patron has less need to fight for power. Without this struggle, it's easier to address the issue.

Remember that emotion is part of many problems

When a patron is yelling about an overdue book he never checked out, we want to work on the overdue and discuss that. Unfortunately, the patron's anger makes that almost impossible, so instead of a dialogue we have two competing monologues, neither accomplishing much. When the anger or other emotion is strong, we have to address that before we can get to the topic. That's where empathy, reflecting, and "I" statements come in. If we choose to ignore the emotion, there will be times when we are simply not going to be heard.

Understand left brain–right brain differences

There is a biological reason that at least partly explains why we can't ignore the emotion in a situation. The human brain is divided into two hemispheres, and scientists are discovering that this is more significant than they realized. The oversimplified explanation is that the right half of the brain deals with emotion and feelings, and the left half processes facts and information. I used to be skeptical about the "right brain–left brain" theory, doubting that it had any relevancy outside of brain surgery. I now swear by it and can see it in action every day. When patrons are upset and emotional, functioning on the right side, it's hard to deal with them on a nonemotional basis. If a friend is pouring out her heart to you about the troubled state of her marriage and you ask her a factual question, such as, "How many years have you two lived in that house together?" you can see a reaction similar to a car going 90 mph, then dropping into reverse. She has to switch to the other half of her brain to get that data, and it can be slower than an old computer going from one program to another. The practical meaning of this is that we have to first deal with a person where he or she is. In the case of someone in an emotional state, we have to do some reflecting and empathy building, allowing the person to calm down, and then we are able to work with facts.

Develop a sense of teamwork with the other person

When you have an unhappy patron, his problem should be your problem. Nothing should be more important to you than working on that issue. Even if it seems petty to you, taking action can make the patron feel you are on his side. If a patron is upset that you don't have a book with a picture of Melvil

Dewey as a baby, walk with the patron and look at a few possible books. If you don't find what he wants and he's still unhappy, write his complaint down, put it in an envelope addressed to the library director, and put it in the outgoing mail pile. Talk with the patron: "I can see you believe this is important. I can't guarantee what our director will do on this, but I can guarantee you that she will know about your issue, okay?" You two are working together toward a common goal. This is a great preventive measure because it's hard to get angry at someone who is working with you. No matter how insignificant the issue is to you, show that you recognize its importance to the patron and will do what you can to help.

Allow five seconds of silence

Those lulls in the conversation can be uncomfortable, and we seek to avoid them, covering them up with babble if necessary. Instead of fighting silence, we should look for ways to use it. When dealing with an emotional crisis, for example, we need to give patrons a chance to vent their feelings. By pausing, even for five seconds, we allow a chance for additional thoughts and feelings to be expressed. We gain more insight.

Silence is also a great way to complete a discussion that needs to be completed. If you have spent some time with a patron who is unhappy about a rule, listened to her concerns, explained the reasons, shown her the policy, explored options, and told her how to take the complaint to the board or the director for further consideration, there is not much left to do. Sometimes, however, the patron still has some fight left in her. She continues to complain, and you say, "As I told you, the director will be happy to look into this for you. I'm sorry, but there's nothing more anyone else can do." *Silence.* If comments continue, you can respond with silence or the briefest acknowledgment, "I understand," followed by more silence. There's nothing left to discuss, and because most people are uncomfortable with silence, it's probably going to make your patron uneasy and ready to leave. It's also useful with the overly talkative patron, after we politely say our good-byes.

Silence is tough for most of us to hear but can be an extremely effective tool to gain more information or to end a discussion.

Ask good questions

The biggest single problem I see in communication in libraries is failing to understand what a patron really wants. We proceed without all the facts and, despite good intentions, give inadequate service. Asking the right questions is a vital tool to gain understanding of a patron's needs. If understanding is a destination, then the right question is our private jet to take us straight there.

You can tell more about a person by the questions he asks than the answers he gives. Questions can give us insight and information. They can also demonstrate that we care and are sensitive to the feelings and concerns of the other person. We don't have to proceed in a conversation without knowing where we are going.

Know your audience
Before you start talking, think about the person with whom you are talking to, what is important to them, and what frame of reference will be familiar. Politicians and marketers spend untold millions to research audiences before shaping their message. We can't do a focus group and an opinion poll before every comment we make, but we can use what we know to put our message in terms that will give us the best chance of being understood.

Know what you want to say before you say it
Pause and gather your thoughts before speaking. Once you've said something, you can't unsay it. There are no "erase and rewind" options in life. Think about your words and tone before speaking. Be sure you understand the person's meaning before answering, or ask a clarifying question. A brief pause to put your thoughts and words in order can save you lots of time and trouble in the long run. That's another reason to be comfortable with silence.

Be open
If you keep your mind open to all kinds of comments, you will improve your ability to understand others. We all know we hear what we want to hear. If we can grow past that habit and hear what the *speaker* wants us to hear, we will take giant strides in communicating. We have to suspend our feelings, judgments, and biases to try to accept the speaker's message. Process it from the speaker's point of view. If we can avoid shutting down or silently defending our views when we hear a message we don't agree with, we can take our communication to a deeper level of understanding. It's a great way to prevent conflict.

Know library policies and departmental services
It's easy to compartmentalize ourselves at the library, becoming experts in our own area and paying little attention to other departments. Let's say you work in the children's room and hear a mother grumbling that all of the particular parenting books she is looking for are unavailable. If you are familiar with interlibrary loan, you can tell her about that service and refer her to the

proper desk. Even though that's "not my department" and the subject may not come up often, your knowledge helped someone find what she was looking for and kept everyone happy. By learning as much as we can about the entire library, we can prevent some problems.

Most people are visual learners

People don't all process information the same way. Some of us do better by hearing, others by reading. Studies show that most people are visual learners, meaning that they have more success processing information they can see. That's why big corporations use elaborate visual aids even when the high-powered presenter can easily give the exact same information verbally. Knowing this, we need to give patrons handouts when we try to explain a policy in question. Take a moment to underline the pertinent points so the patron will be sure to see them.

Assess your communication

We should always be trying to become better communicators, at the library and in our everyday lives. Ask for feedback from coworkers after you've just had a tough encounter with a patron. Find out how they interpreted your responses and listening skills. Ask questions: "I think that last guy was mostly upset about the new video policy. Is that what you thought he was getting at?" "Did what I told him make sense? I'm not sure he really got my point." "How do you explain that rule?" and "I was getting frustrated after awhile. Could you tell it in my voice?" Do an inventory of the entire event. Think about ways you can improve, but also look at what went right in the conversation.

Ask yourself three main questions:

1. What else could I have done to listen and understand the patron's point of view?
2. How could I have responded better?
3. What did I do that worked best?

This checks your listening and observational performance as well as your delivery skills. If a conversation went poorly, try to identify the exact point where things went wrong. Usually when communication goes awry there was one critical misunderstanding that made the difference: a misinterpreted word, an unclear phrase, an overlooked message, a wrong tone of voice, something missed or misstated.

Here's an example of assessing our communication skills. A mother in the children's room was grumbling about "all these books about sex in the kids' area. What ever happened to the books we read as kids?" I took the patron over to a section of "classics" and said "Here are some books you might enjoy. Let me know if you need help finding anything else." The mother left a few minutes later without taking any of the books and with a very unhappy look on her face.

When I talked to a coworker who was nearby, she said the patron seemed pretty upset about the library owning some of those controversial "sex books." That observation clued me in to the entire problem. The critical point in this case was when I chose to focus on finding the "books like we used to read" rather than talk about the controversial books we own. Those books were really the main focus for the patron, but I overlooked it even though it is a valid concern. My decision to find the other books was natural because most of us want to avoid the negative. I could have prevented this problem by (1) listening to the tone of her voice, (2) being open to hearing something I didn't want to hear, and (3) directly addressing the "sex books" statement. I should have questioned the patron about what she wanted me to do: "You seem concerned about these books on sex in the children's section. Would you like to talk to the manager of our children's room?" By allowing her to answer, she would have felt listened to and respected. I would be sure that I was responding to the *real* needs of this patron, not my *perception* of her needs. By analyzing this little situation, I can be better prepared to handle the next situation.

Make communication a priority

At work and in the rest of our lives, our success with people is determined by our ability to communicate as much as any other reason. We can influence this greatly simply by deciding it is important to communicate better and making an ongoing effort. Listening, accepting other ideas, and speaking clearly and openly can help us. In many cases we have the skills but need to add the willingness. Recognizing that other people want to be heard and understood as much as we do is a good start. Committing to helping others be understood is a decision that can change our lives, at the library and beyond. Communication is that powerful.

17

How You Say It Matters

Jerry is house-sitting for Joe while Joe's on an extended trip. Joe calls to check on his home. "How's everything going?" he asks.

"Well, your dog died," Jerry says.

"That's terrible!" says Joe. "You should break it to me more gently. Next time tell me 'Your dog is on the roof.' Then, the next time I call, say, 'The dog fell off the roof.' Then tell me, 'He's at the vet; I'm not sure if he'll make it,' and then you can tell me the dog died. Break it to me gradually."

"You're right. Sorry," says Jerry.

"That's okay. Any other news?" asks Joe.

"Well," Jerry says, "your mother is on the roof."

This story illustrates the basic point of this chapter—it's not just what you say, it's also how you say it. We often have to give patrons unwelcome news—they have outstanding fines, the book isn't available, they can't check out a reference book, and so forth. If we deliver the message poorly, we increase the chances of having to face an angry, irate patron. If we deliver it properly, we can often prevent that problem. Because we would rather prevent problems than deal with them, it makes sense that we spend some time deciding how to break unwelcome news.

The first step is to always keep your patron in mind. Even if we have to tell patrons they have too many overdues dozens of times a day, it may be the first time that a specific patron has heard that. This patron doesn't necessarily know what that means, what the consequences are, and what he or she should do about this new situation.

Here are a few basic tips to help the library staff and the patron:

Don't make it personal
Instead of saying "You can't check out anything. You've got too many overdues. I can't check these out for you," try saying "The computer says you have three books overdue, and our policy does not allow anything to be checked out until these are returned. Do you want me to find out what items are listed as overdue?" Now it's the overdues, the computer, and the library policies that are the issues. It's not you versus the patron. Everything is on a factual level; nothing is personal or accusatory.

Suggest alternatives
Rather than "You can't check that out. It's a reference book," try "Reference books are not to be checked out. I can check and see if we have a copy that is in our circulating collection." It's not fair to expect the patron to know what the options are. How would the average Joe know that we sometimes get several copies and make one reference and let the others circulate? Or that last year's edition has been moved from reference to circulating? We may not be able to find a suitable replacement, but helping patrons look at options at least helps them realize that we are trying and are on their side. There's nothing worse than a "you can't do that" followed by an icy stare and silence.

Say "I'm sorry"
This does not imply that it's your fault; it simply acknowledges that you realize that this isn't working the way the patron hoped and you regret any inconvenience. It's part of that human equation that goes on in all our transactions, whether we realize it or not.

Be willing to explain why
If you don't allow a reference book to go out, be sure the customer understands why this can't be done. If you see a quizzical look on the patron's face, give an explanation of the reasons for this policy.

Avoid contradicting the patron

Let's say your customer is checking out a book and argues, "They always let me have it for five weeks! When did you start this three-week checkout?" You will set up an unnecessary confrontation if you say, "I'm sorry, we never allow books out for five weeks. You must be thinking of some other library." Now you have directly contradicted the patron, and some people will feel challenged and respond defensively. Avoid that by saying, "We went to a three-week loan period several years ago, so anyone giving something differently made a mistake. I'm sorry about the confusion." We know that in all probability the patron never received a book from our library for five weeks. There's seldom any value in arguing to prove that, however. We're better off just to state what the current policy is, apologize for any misunderstanding, and move ahead.

You can actually take this "how you say it" approach a step further and help the entire library. Develop a simple manual to help all staff learn ways to break the news in common situations. This is something that requires no cost except a little time and effort. It can pay off big in prevention of problems. Here's the process:

Goal

Create a Customer Service Language Manual, which will give staff options when they have to give unpleasant news to patrons.

Guidelines

Brainstorm typical situations

Ask staff to come up with the policies and situations that are toughest for them to discuss with patrons. This can be done as a large group, small groups, or even as a write-in. Be sure that they realize that you are asking this with the purpose of devising some ways to make this part of their job easier. Is it overdues, fines owed, video limits, Internet time restrictions, problems with reserves, or what? The list has to cite what is important to those frontline staff who have to present this information to patrons. If they agree that it is awkward and they know of no good way to tell a patron he owes $12 in fines, then that has to be a topic for later discussion. Don't go into this process with any preconceived notions. Let the process work.

Develop a committee

Assemble a committee of staff who deal with patrons on a regular basis. Include a variety of levels of staff from circulation, reference, and any other group that deal regularly with the public. Look for your best, most enthusiastic staff for this. Be sure to include some newer staff and some who have experience at other libraries. (In a very small library, consider doing this jointly with another small library nearby. You want to have enough people on your committee to generate some enthusiasm.) Present them with the list of concerns.

Choose the top problems and best approaches

Ask the committee to prioritize the top five or six problem areas and reach a consensus that these are the biggest challenges. Then, start a brainstorming session on ways to present these in a more positive manner. Ask if committee members have any tried-and-true methods. Use ideas from this book and other library training manuals to help. Typically, you'll find that someone has an approach that others like, and someone will say, "Gee, I wish I had said that the other day."

List suggested responses

Create a list of possible responses to various situations. Be sure staff realize these are just options. We don't want to turn library staff into fast-food-service robots who automatically ask "You want fries with those books?" These are suggestions they can use or put into words they are most comfortable with.

Polish and publish your manual

Get some reviews. Show the initial list to some frontline staff and see what they think. Find out if the language sounds natural enough and if staff believe this wording will help. Let some of your committee members try the suggestions with real live patrons and see how they work. Edit and revise as necessary based on your test run and comments. Prepare your manual, and distribute it to all appropriate staff. An example of this type of manual is in appendix 4.

Train staff

You can really reinforce the ideas by doing some training. Have members of the original committee present these ideas at a staff meeting. Try role-playing where a staff member says something terribly wrong, and the staff member playing the patron responds horribly. Then, use the new ideas from the manual and show that the results are a little piece of heaven on Earth. You can also draft volunteers from the training group to participate. A short training session such as this will multiply the odds of staff actually reading and using the manual.

Such role-playing gives staff practical guidance and experience, both of which apply specifically to their daily problems. The process here does not have to be followed exactly, but the crucial element is staff involvement—in identifying the difficult situations and coming up with improved responses.

We have a choice of using words that will build connections or walls. How we choose will strongly influence the kind of relationships we have with our customers. A positive statement will have a better chance of getting positive results. I'm positive!

Saying It and Meaning It Exercise

This exercise lists expressions of negative and corresponding positive statements. Think of other situations that offer us a choice of positive and negative comments. Look for the best and worst way to make these comments.

LOSERS

"That's not my job."

"I don't know."

"That's not my department—try upstairs."

"What?"

"I don't make the rules; I just do as I'm told."

"We've always done it that way."

WINNERS

"I don't know, but I'll find out for you."

"I think that's handled by our business office, upstairs. Let me call and check first."

"I'm not sure if that rule is a problem. I don't have the authority to change it, but you can talk to my supervisor."

"It's not in right now. I can put a reserve on it or see if we can get it from interlibrary loan."

"That's our current policy, but I can ask the director to reconsider it."

"Does that completely answer your question?"

"Is there anything else I can do for you?"

"*Thank you.*"

18

An Ounce of Prevention

Sometimes there is nothing we can do to prevent a problem. Someone has a bad day and wanders into the library like a grumpy bear waking from hibernation. The best we can do in this case is to provide our usual great service and avoid poking the bear. If any problems do arise, we use our best people skills and try to resolve it as best we can.

If we really do some soul searching, however, we will admit that we sometimes cause problems. Maybe we aren't completely to blame, but we make missteps that transform a teddy bear into a snarling grizzly. Here's a classic, and true, example.

Situation of the Day

A young man (we'll call him Fred) was trying to bring his bike into the library when a guard informed him that bikes are not allowed. The guard pointed to the bike rack in the back. The young man protested, saying he had no lock. The guard stuck to the policy, so Fred left his bike at the rack, figuring he was only running in for a minute. When he completed his business and returned to the bike rack, there was only empty space where his bike had been.

Fred was understandably upset and went to tell the guard. The guard told him to use the pay phone and call the police and that there was nothing the guard could do. Fred said he didn't have any money. The guard pointed to a reference desk and said, "Maybe they will let you use the phone," and walked away.

Fred went over to the desk and explained the situation. The reference librarian said the phone at that desk was for staff use only and pointed Fred to the information desk.

Growing more upset by the minute, Fred went to the information desk, where he repeated his story. The librarian at the information desk directed Fred to the circulation desk, where he once again had to repeat his story and request to use a phone to call the police. By this time, poor Fred sounded extremely irate and frustrated, so some kind soul took pity on Fred and let him use the staff phone. Unfortunately, the kind soul walked off to some other task. Another staff person walked by and saw this strange nonstaffer talking excitedly on the staff phone and immediately started questioning him about why he was on the phone, interrupting his conversation with the police.

By now, Fred was nearly hysterical and responded to the staff member in a rather loud and harsh voice. The supervisor, in his office behind the desk, heard a patron yell at a staff member but couldn't make out what was said. The loud tones concerned the supervisor, who valiantly went to the staff member's rescue. The supervisor told Fred he could not talk to library staff like that, that the phones were for staff use only, and that Fred needed to get off the phone.

Fred was now beyond angry words at what seemed to be a conspiracy to keep him from reporting his stolen bike to the police. Losing all control, Fred hurled the nearest book at the supervisor, who was saved by the fact that Fred's anger had cost him his ability to aim. The supervisor called the guard to have Fred removed from the library because he had thrown a book at a library staff member.

Needless to say, it took quite some time to get this all straightened out, and Fred still has not sent in his "Friends of the Library" membership.

What Went Wrong?

Certainly, Fred was wrong to yell and to throw a book. Also, we could reasonably argue that if he had a bike lock, maybe all of this would have been avoided. However, if we are willing to look for ways to reduce problems at libraries we can also use this example to see lots of mistakes by the library.

What went wrong? The easy answer is *everything*, but let's dig a little deeper and make a list:

Lack of training on library policy
This library has a policy that states that "any reasonable request for assistance should be granted to a patron who has been the victim of crime." Clearly, the policymakers wanted the library staff to allow someone in Fred's situation to use a staff phone to call the police. The guard and staff did not know the policy, possibly because they had not been trained on it.

Failure to use good judgment on applying policies
Even if staff did not know the policy that allowed crime victims to use the phone, they should have realized that they have the flexibility to apply the policy in a wise and reasonable manner. Either they did not receive training that informed them of their ability to use their judgment in unusual situations such as this or they failed to use that discretion. Staff need to be told explicitly by administration that they have flexibility in applying policy, especially in very unusual cases. Administration then must back up staff who use their judgment in cases like this.

The customer was shuffled around
The angriest people I have ever had to deal with have always been people who have been sent from office to office, usually with casual comments such as, "I don't know who does that. Try the social sciences desk." Not only does this waste the customer's time, but it also shows an indifference toward their needs. If you don't know where to send a person, call and find out first. It only takes a minute on the phone to say, "I have a customer here who wants to see about interlibrary loan. Are you the person he should talk to?" This shows you are trying to give the best service you can, alerts your coworker of a question, and teaches you one more fact about how your place of employment works. It also avoids creating an angry bear for someone to deal with.

In the case of Fred, or anyone who is upset or having a problem, it's even better if you can walk him to where he needs to go and be sure that he gets his issue addressed. The guard or the first librarian who had contact with Fred should have volunteered to take him to where he could make a call and be sure he was taken care of. A staff member walking Fred to a desk and saying "He needs to use our phone to call the police. It's an emergency. Is it okay if he uses yours?" would have prevented much of this unhappy situation. Sometimes it means leaving a desk unattended for a few minutes, but think of all the time that would have saved everyone in this particular case.

Poor interpersonal skills

All the people involved failed to listen to Fred's situation and see things from his point of view, as we discussed earlier. They may have heard the words "I need to use the phone to call the police," but no one heard his frustration and anger. We don't have to be psychologists but we do have to be human in our jobs. We are in a people business.

Lack of teamwork

It's bad etiquette to send a snarling bear to an unsuspecting coworker. We are all in this together and need to realize the consequence of our actions, or inactions, on our coworkers.

We will always have to face difficult people from time to time in any public-service job.

The good news is that we can reduce the number significantly by taking four reasonable steps:

1. Develop good policies.

2. Train the staff in the policies and how to apply them.

3. Apply the policies in a wise and reasonable manner.

4. Inform the public of your policies.

19

Good Policies
Make Good Patrons

In our jobs, we have personnel manuals, employee handbooks, collections of memos, maybe a union agreement, and lots of other pieces of paper to explain our parameters. They tell us what we can and can't do, how long our breaks are, and what behavior is expected.

Customers need the same guidelines (with maybe fewer memos). That's why every library needs some type of rules for the public. Patrons need to know what they can and can't do. These days most libraries have some sort of document like this, but don't assume that *any* is better than none. Your "Rules for Patrons" is an important document and needs to be treated as such. Let's look at some keys to developing good rules.

Keys to Good Rules

Must be clear
An average person reading the rules should understand them without any help. That means avoiding any jargon or library slang. Short, simple, and to the point is the only way to go here.

Easy to explain

Every staff member should be able to give an example of what sort of behavior a given rule is meant to address. The public should be able to think of examples also.

Easy to justify

If someone asks, "Why do you have a rule against that?" everyone on the staff should know why and be able to answer. So if you get asked, "Why can't I wear my rollerblades in the library?" you should be able to respond, "We allowed them for a while and learned that they damage the floor, and we had complaints about the noise they make. Also, if anyone falls while wearing them, they could really get hurt or knock someone else down. We would have injured customers and maybe a lawsuit, so the board made a rule against wearing rollerblades in the library."

If you can't justify the rule in a clear manner that the average person would understand, then the rule needs to be rethought.

Legal

We want our rules to be enforceable, which means they must pass a reasonable legal review. Although everything is open to court challenge these days, a reasonable review by the appropriate legal experts is a necessary step. It shows diligence and gives the library a layer of protection, even if it's not perfect protection.

Really needed

Examine every rule or proposed rule. Be sure it benefits the staff and public. Remember that each rule you create gives staff more to police. Ask yourself, "What would happen if we didn't have this rule? Is it creating more hassle than it's worth?" Rules are only necessary to help run a smooth, safe, and efficient library. If a rule doesn't contribute to those causes, banish it. Everyone has enough to do without enforcing extra rules.

Reasonably specific

A vague rule is impossible to enforce, doesn't give the public any real guidance, and will cause staff untold headaches. If we post a rule that says "No troublemaking," we have succeeded in being concise but failed to do much else. Additionally, it opens staff up to charges of uneven enforcement, because one person's definition of troublemaking may be very different from someone else's. That will lead to complaints, staff disagreements, and possible legal actions.

Made known to the public

Post your rules in a prominent place, near the entrance or checkout desk. Have copies available as handouts.

Writing Your Rules

Almost every library today has a list of "Rules for Patrons." When did you last review yours carefully? If it's been more than a year or if you think they can be improved, let's go over them right now. I'll wait while you dig them out. By the way, if it takes more than two minutes or two people to find them, that's a problem that will need to be addressed.

Set this goal: have as few rules as possible. You should be able to print them on one page (no fair using type too small to read or poster-sized pages).

Because most of the library staff will be involved in dealing with these rules in one way or another, you should have a staff committee to create or revise these rules. The committee should consist of staff from all levels, from frontline, entry-level circulation staffers to administration. It's really useful to have new staff members involved in undertakings such as these because they have not yet learned all your organizational culture and can bring fresh perspectives.

Convene your staff committee, order the pizza, and set up the flip chart and easel. While they are eating the pizza, be sure staff understand the goal of one-page maximum and are familiar with the guidelines for making good rules. Instead of starting by reading your current rules and asking, "Is everyone happy with rule number one?" start completely fresh, as if there had never been a rules document in your library.

Ask "What are your biggest concerns?" Think about safety of staff and patrons and ways to make the library more efficient and pleasant for all. Be sure the group knows that it is okay to toss out more ideas than you will ultimately be able to use.

After compiling this master list, it's time to combine and edit. Prioritize issues that really make a difference for staff and patrons as compared to those that are just our personal issues or rules we have had since the beginning of time. Don't worry too much about precise wording yet. Depending on the size of your group and your library, it may be a good idea to end your first session with a preliminary draft that is longer than the final can be. Show this around to staff and see what opinions you get. Especially try to get an idea of which ones are most important.

When it comes time to edit, delete rules pertaining to uncommon situations. Such rules may not need to be spelled out specifically. It's a good idea to have some general statement about "actions not appropriate for the library environment" and this statement can cover those unusual situations.

Some sample policies are included in appendix 5. Use these to get ideas of wording and to see if you have missed anything. Prepare a final draft that fits on one page and is acceptable to the committee and staff. Check each rule against the guidelines to be sure it is necessary, clear, explainable, and easily understood by anyone who reads it. It's a good idea to show it to a few nonlibrary friends or family members to see if they understand every word of it. See if these outside people have any questions or comments.

After the director has agreed to these rules, it is now time for the *dreaded* legal review. I say *dreaded* because this is where your hard work can come under its greatest threat—legalese! Brief your lawyer in advance of the goals your library has set, especially regarding overall length and simplicity. Be prepared for some give and take. If your lawyer rewrites something that you feel does not meet your goal, go back and work with him. Find out why the lawyer rewrote a rule, and see if you can offer a compromise that addresses this concern yet meets your goals as well. Work together until you can come up with a revision that is acceptable to the party of the first part as well as the party of the second part. If you hit a really serious impasse, see if you can get another lawyer to help you reach an "out-of-court settlement."

Once your rules are written, fit on one page, and are approved by the lawyers, it's time to get approval from the board of trustees (city council or other supervising body for your library). Be sure the board understands what the rules are, how you arrived at them, and how they will be enforced. It's crucial that the board officially adopts the rules and that the official version you post has the board approval date clearly showing. With this stamp of approval, the library staff is never in the position of defending the policies. Staff must be able to explain why the rules were created, but once they have been approved by the board, the staff does not have to defend them. Anyone who feels a rule should be changed is referred to the director and the board, getting staff out of the middle of a situation they can't change anyway.

Once approved, the next step is to make people aware of the rules. Secret rules do no good. With our convenient one-page size, we can post it easily. Even though you now have a wonderful set of rules, it's still not a good idea to put them everyplace. An unobtrusive posting by each entrance and maybe one by the information or circulation desk are plenty. No matter how many signs you have posted, people will only read so many of them. You have to choose carefully what you want your public to read and prioritize. Just because you have put up more signs does not mean you have done more communication—it often means just the opposite.

Be sure you have plenty of copies available to hand out when you need to remind someone of the rules. It's much easier to say, "I'm sorry. Our board of trustees has a policy prohibiting soliciting in the library. Here's a copy of the rules. You may want to take a look at it. Thanks for your cooperation," and hand out the rules. Be sure all staff know where the copies are and how to get more when supplies run low.

20

Policy Training

Now that we have those great rules approved, printed on pretty paper, and posted, we're done, right? Wrong, of course! We have to be sure staff are trained to understand and enforce the rules.

Staff need to know

exactly what the rules are;

why each rule exists so they can explain and answer questions;

what each staff member's role in enforcement is;

what the roles of others (including guards, police officers, supervisors, etc.) are; and

how much discretion each staff member has in enforcing the rules and dealing with unusual circumstances.

The best way to educate staff is with a face-to-face training session with each staff member. When your board passes a new set of rules, a training program needs to be quickly created and implemented. A reasonable start is to train all existing staff and set regular training for new staff members. Work on a written outline to review each rule, what it means, and how to enforce it. The sample in figure 20.1 is based on my own set of "ideal" rules. (Additional patron conduct policies are in appendix 5.)

Rules of Conduct

Welcome to your public library. We want to offer the best service possible to library visitors in a pleasant environment. Each person can help by following these rules:

1. Eating and drinking are prohibited, except in the Community Room during scheduled events.
2. All children must be supervised. Children under the age of seven must be under the direct supervision of a person over the age of thirteen.
3. The following are not permitted in the library:

   - weapons
   - sleeping
   - use of tobacco
   - begging, soliciting, or sales
   - animals, except guide dogs and other assistive animals
   - abusive, threatening, or obscene language

4. Damage or destruction of library property is a crime and will be prosecuted to the fullest extent of the law.
5. Shirt, shoes, and appropriate clothing are required.
6. Quiet conversation is allowed as long as it does not disturb others.
7. Bathing or shaving in library facilities is prohibited.
8. Persons under the influence of drugs or alcohol or illegal drugs are not permitted in the library.
9. Persons who pose a health or sanitary risk will be asked to leave.

Library management reserves the right to expel anyone whose behavior is disruptive, is inappropriate for the library environment, or interferes with the use of the library by other patrons. If you see anyone violating one of these rules, please contact a staff member immediately. Thank you!

Approved by
your public library
Board of Trustees, Nov. 22, 1999

FIGURE 20.1   Sample policy

Note: rules need to be different in different libraries. It's not a good idea simply to adopt these or other preexisting rules. Additionally, the process of developing rules with input from all levels of staff is crucial and must not be skipped. The staff members who deal with the rules on a daily basis cannot be left out of the development stage.

Staff Training

Training on the rules can be done in an hour or so, time well spent considering the problems this training can help us avoid. The director or another administrator (or a training specialist if your library is lucky enough to have one) can walk a group of employees through the rules, giving background and answering questions. An outline will help ensure consistent training from one session to the next. Working with the above set as an example, here's a sample training course on these rules:

Sample Training Course

Today we are going to go over the rules for patrons here at your library. Each of you needs to understand these rules, why we have them, and what your role is in enforcing them. Some of these rules deal with circumstances you are unlikely to have to deal with, such as drugs or weapons, but we want to be sure you know what to do if these situations ever come up when you're working. Most of the time you will deal with the routine rules, such as no eating or no loud conversations.

Before we review each of these specific rules, here are a few general points:

> You need to know and understand these rules. If a patron asks why we have a rule, you should be able to give a simple, reasonable answer. It is fine a patron asks such a question. If the patron disagrees with a rule and feels it should be changed, all you have to say is, "These rules have been approved by our board of trustees, and I don't have the authority to change them. I can get our director or you can attend our board meeting, which is held on the third Tuesday of every month at 4:00 P.M. in the Community Room." You don't have to defend the rules.

> You have the authority to call the police any time you think it is necessary. You do not need to wait to get the okay from a supervisor. If you see a situation that could be dangerous to staff or patrons, call 911 immediately. After you place the call, notify the supervisor and

---

guards that you have called and why so they will not be surprised when the police show up. If it turns out that nothing happens, that's fine. It's better to be safe than sorry, and administration will fully support you any time you call the police for a potential emergency.

You have the right to use some professional judgment in enforcing these rules. Remember that the rules exist only to help us operate the library in a safe, efficient manner. If bending a rule prevents more problems than enforcing the rule creates, then it makes sense to bend the rule. If you can't get a supervisor, you can make these decisions on your own. The bottom line is that you want to do what is in the best interest of the library and patrons.

You can enforce most of these rules with a simple three-strikes approach. The first step is to let the patrons know they are breaking a rule and give them a copy of our rules.

The second step is to warn them that this is their second notice, and if they continue to break the rules, they will have to leave the library. On the third occasion, tell them to leave. If they refuse, call the police and the patrons can be charged with criminal trespassing. Let them know that you will call the police. A few rules have some special enforcement approaches, and we'll cover those as we go through.

Let's review each of the rules:

1. *Eating and drinking are prohibited, except in the Community Room during scheduled events.*

    This can lead to spills, which can damage materials, carpet, and tables. We don't have an adequate maintenance staff to clean up.

    To use the Community Room, groups must be nonprofit and schedule at the information desk.

    A good approach is to take a trash can to the table and say, "Eating is not allowed in the library. Can I help you dispose of that?" If they want to eat, let them know that you can hold their books while they go outside and finish.

2. *All children must be supervised. Children under the age of seven must be under the direct supervision of a person over the age of thirteen.*

    The library staff cannot watch children. It's too easy for children to wander out of the building or be taken by a stranger and we would never know. Parents wouldn't leave their young children unattended in a mall, and it's no safer to leave them unattended in a library.

    By "direct supervision" we mean that the parent or guardian must be able to see the child. If they are in different rooms, there is no direct supervision. If the parents are in the Community Room, they are not supervising their child. For example, if you see a little girl who seems to be under the age of seven, approach the child, let her know that you work at the library, and ask her age. If she is under seven, help her to find her parent, and give the parent a copy of the rules.

If the parent continues to leave the child, let the parent know the second time that he will be asked to leave the library if it happens again. Then, using the three-strikes approach, we have to ask the parent to leave on the third violation.

If a child under the age of seven is at the library alone, talk to the child and try to contact a parent or guardian to come pick up the child. If you cannot reach anyone, call the police. Stay with the child until the police arrive.

3. *The following are not permitted in the library:*

- *weapons*

   If you see anyone with a knife, gun, or other weapon, call the police.

- *sleeping*

   Sleeping is not allowed because it is inappropriate for a library and takes up space that could be used by patrons doing library work. If you see someone sleeping, *do not touch him or her.* Say, "Excuse me; sleeping is not allowed in the library." If the patron does not wake up, tap on the desk and repeat the message. If you cannot wake him or her that way, he or she may be ill, and you should call 911.

- *use of tobacco*

   Smoking and chewing tobacco are against local ordinances. Smoking is allowed outside, near the ash can.

- *begging, soliciting, or sales*

   These things disturb other patrons who are trying to study and also can intimidate them so they are not allowed.

- *animals, except guide dogs and other assistive animals*

   Pets can make a mess and some patrons are allergic to animals.

- *abusive, threatening, or obscene language*

   Patrons should not be subjected to this sort of treatment at the library. This is a little tricky to deal with because it's not always clear what constitutes these types of language. Any time a patron complains that another patron has used such language toward or around him or her, take the patron's word for it.

   Staff do not have to tolerate abusive treatment from the public either. You will sometimes have to accept some rudeness, but you are not here to be abused. If you feel language used toward you or other staff is harassing or abusive, tell the patron that this kind of language is not acceptable in the library. If he continues, let him know you will help him with his library issues, but you cannot help until he uses language appropriate for the library. If it continues, the patron can be asked to leave, just as if he broke any other rule. Another option is to get a supervisor to talk to the patron after the first warning, but if that's not possible, it's perfectly legitimate to have a patron leave for abusive language toward staff.

4. *Damage or destruction of library property is a crime and will be prosecuted to the fullest extent of the law.*

It's pretty obvious that we must protect property paid for by tax money. To enforce this, be observant. For example, if you see a businesswoman take some magazines to a table and pull scissors out of a briefcase, that's when you need to take action. Alert a coworker or a guard and go over near the patron. You may even ask if she is finding everything she needs, but be sure she realizes she is being watched. If you believe the patron has destroyed any property or may be dangerous, call the police. If the patron leaves before the police arrive, get a description, and, if you can, get a license plate number. *Remember, never place yourself in any danger.*

5. *Shirt, shoes, and appropriate clothing are required.*

This is partly for the safety of patrons and partly to keep an appropriate environment.

6. *Quiet conversation is allowed as long as it does not disturb others.*

We don't require silence, but noise that disturbs others makes it impossible for them to use the library.

If you can hear a conversation from a few feet away, it's probably too loud. If a patron complains, let the talkers know that their conversation is disturbing others and give them a copy of the rules. Then follow the three-strikes approach.

7. *Bathing or shaving in library facilities is prohibited.*

This is both unsanitary and inappropriate.

8. *Persons under the influence of drugs or alcohol or illegal drugs are not permitted in the library.*

Besides being illegal, it is dangerous and disruptive to the other patrons. People in this condition are to leave the library immediately—no warnings given. Be extremely careful approaching anyone who you think may be under the influence. Even if the patron seems pleasant, drugs or alcohol can lead to sudden and violent mood changes. Never approach someone you suspect of drug or alcohol use alone. Don't hesitate to call the police.

9. *Persons who pose a health or sanitary risk will be asked to leave.*

This deals mostly with people who smell bad, because offensive odor prevents others from using the library. If you get a complaint from a patron or you are disturbed by someone's body odor, then it means people cannot use the library in the manner it is intended. Give a copy of the rules to the person and ask him or her to leave. There are no three-strikes on this one. Be sure all these patrons know they are welcome back once they have cleaned up, and help them get information about social services, which offer such assistance as showers, overnight shelter, or clean clothes. Some people might not even be aware that they smell bad; others might suffer from a physical condition that makes it difficult for them to want to be clean. Regardless, they should be treated with respect. We can try to help them get to the appropriate services, but they cannot stay in the library if they prevent other people from using our services.

No matter how many rules we write, we can never cover all the possible situations. We can write a rule that says "no radios," and patrons will believe they are not breaking the rules when they come in with a portable TV. For this last rule, you have to use your best judgment to be sure that we provide a safe, pleasant environment for our patrons. The bottom line is that any patron behavior that interferes with the ability of patrons to use the library or staff to do their jobs is prohibited. You have to remember that.

Now that we've finished going over the specific rules, we can close by remembering why we have rules.

You have to understand our rules and explain why we have them. You do not have to defend them. Send those patrons who want to change a rule to the director or encourage them to attend a board meeting.

Use the three-strikes approach with most infractions. If anyone seems dangerous, you do not have to give him or her a warning before asking him or her to leave.

You have the authority to call the police if you see a potentially dangerous situation. Don't wait to call. After you call the police, notify your supervisor so the police visit won't be a surprise.

Be sure your training has plenty of time for questions and discussions. Keep an open mind to new ideas from the staff and be willing to revise your training when new problems and solutions come up. Make the tone as upbeat and positive as possible.

The Deluxe Training Program

You can go even further in your training program, creating a manual that gives specific problem situations and a range of responses. This goes beyond just the rule breakers and advises on responses to all kinds of situations. The advantage is that staff always have a guideline for almost any problem. There can be a disadvantage if training and manuals get too specific, and we use them as a substitute for good judgment.

The best example of a detailed situation-training manual is the one used by the Ontario (Calif.) City Library. In addition to listing lots of possible situations, this manual also gives the local or state law that pertains to the situation. A sample section is included in appendix 6.

Although the Ontario manual is a great example, it is absolutely crucial that each library develops its own guidelines and manuals. We all have unique communities, buildings, staff, and needs. Additionally, the process is as important as the result. If we take the policies from another library and adopt them entirely, we will be able to check an item off our to-do list, but we will lose the experience of creating the policies. Although it might not sound exciting, the discussion, thought process, research, and other work that goes into making a thorough set of operating procedures are extremely valuable. This process is an opportunity for staff from all levels to work together, share ideas and concerns, and create a product they can call their own. We can also call on community organizations to assist, adding to our knowledge of local resources and building ongoing connections.

We all are more willing to adopt rules we help make than ones lifted from outside, no matter how good those are. Equally important, all those sessions to create our new policies offered plenty of excuses to order pizza.

21

Helping the Security Force Help You

For him that stealeth a book from this library, let it change into a serpent in his hand and rend him . . .

—Sixteenth-century curse against book stealers, printed on a sign posted at the monastery of San Pedro, Barcelona

Build a Relationship with the Police

Sometimes we have to look to more contemporary solutions in dealing with crime in the library. We all know that in an emergency we can call the police. Should our only dealing with the police be after we dial 911? If you have any trouble ever at your library, you should be talking to the police on a regular basis, not just in an emergency. It's to your advantage and helps the police if you build an ongoing relationship where you both understand how each other works.

Because libraries are such open facilities, we attract all kinds of people. Most get along but typically a few don't, and we need the police to help us. Maybe you have noticed more vagrants hanging out, and a few times the staff have felt threatened. Or possibly vandalism inside and outside the building has been on the rise. That's an opportunity to invite representatives from the local police department to come to the library and discuss your problems. It's best to do this when it's not an emergency.

Meet with the Police

Ideally, a meeting would include administration and some of the frontline staff who regularly see the problem. Others, such as building maintenance staff, may need to be there too, especially if there has been vandalism. Library staff should explain what kinds of problems have occurred, how the library has handled problems so far, and whether there have been any changes recently; staff should also describe any reports made to the police and how the police have responded. Especially let them know about any problems you have not been able to resolve. If you think increased police walk-throughs would help, let them know.

Ask for their advice and take notes. This is their business, and often you can get some good ideas. I have found that the police are realistic and will gladly let you know what has worked and what hasn't. They are also realistic about what they can and can't do.

If you have a specific individual or individuals who have been causing concerns, point them out to the police. Often they know them and can give you an idea of how much of a problem they can be. Sometimes, just having a police officer chat briefly with the person helps. It shows that the library is serious about security and lets the person know he or she is identified. That can be enough to improve behavior or to move the person to another spot. I hate to think how much of what we call *crime prevention* is really *crime relocation*.

Take Crime-Prevention Steps

Many police departments have personal-safety classes and crime-prevention programs. Services range from a brief lecture on how to keep from becoming a victim to a detailed analysis of your facility with recommendations on ways to improve safety. These suggestions, by the way, are not always expensive. Sometimes it is a matter of moving a few items to improve sight lines or adding a crash bar to an exit. Explore the programs offered in your community and take advantage of them. You'll get the benefit of the real-world experience the police offer. Additionally, you'll build a stronger connection between your two organizations, which can help in the future.

Establish a Police Drop-in Center

If you want to go a step further in building this relationship, consider using your library as a drop-in center for the police. If the police who serve your library are not near their headquarters, you can offer to serve as a "home away from home" for them. The idea is that oftentimes the police would like someplace they can do paperwork and maybe make a call or two without returning all the way to the precinct. If your library is in the right location, you can provide that space. In return, you get additional police presence and a good working relationship with the police.

Check with the police and see if they are interested in such an arrangement. If so, dedicate some quiet space or office to this purpose. All it takes are a few supplies and a little space. Be sure they either have coffee there or easy access to an office coffee supply. This should be pleasant space for them. This concept isn't necessary or suitable for every library. If, however, you feel the need for an increased police presence, the drop-in center is an idea to consider.

Hire Security Guards

Sometimes a drop-in presence isn't enough. Your library may need to hire security guards. The presence of a uniform makes a huge difference, helping patrons and staff to feel safer. We have to realize the difference is mostly psychological and that private security guards are not going to stop a major crime. They can prevent plenty of minor crimes, such as vandalism and petty thefts, but that is as much as we should reasonably expect. Perception is important and worth plenty.

Role of the Guards

1. Enforce library policies on proper behavior.
2. Watch for potential crimes to property or people.
3. Notify police in emergencies. Work with police when they arrive.

4. Talk with staff about any security concerns. Staff must be comfortable alerting guards when they feel a potential problem exists.
5. Be highly visible and able to talk to people in a polite but firm manner.

Train Security Guards

When hiring an outside company to provide security, you cannot expect that the company will handle all the work for you. Even if the company recruits, trains, licenses, and pays the guards, your library still has plenty to do. You need to do some training about your specific purposes. That doesn't mean simply showing which key goes to which door. The guards will be called on to enforce your policies, so they need to understand them. Like staff, they also need to understand the enforcement policies and how to apply them. The guards are often the ones to call the police, so they need to know the procedure. Do they only call the police in an emergency but let administration call for vandalism and other nonemergency situations? Whom do they notify when they do call the police? Contract guards start with the disadvantage of not knowing staff. They need to be told who is responsible for making which decisions. It's unfair to a guard to be caught in between two staffers if there is a disagreement. Guards from the outside should have one staff member with primary responsibility for overseeing all aspects of their work and should know whom to go to when that person is not available.

When guards are brought into a library, staff also need to be trained in what responsibilities belong to the guard and what remain with the staff. In most cases, staff need to know that they should still call the police first in any dangerous or emergency situation. If several large guys are getting ready to rumble in the library, one or two guards are unlikely to be able to contain the situation. The guards would see the situation and just call the police anyway, so it makes more sense to get the police on the way as the very first course of action. Calling the guards, who will simply call the police anyway, wastes precious moments in an emergency. Staff need to know when they should call the police and when they should notify the guards. Normally, the guards are notified first except in any situation where there may be risk to the safety of staff or patrons.

In some cases it may not be necessary to go through the expense of hiring guards on a long-term basis. Sometimes a month or two of increased security will chase away the problem patrons.

Off-Duty Police

If you have a real safety concern, private security guards may not be adequate. Give serious consideration to hiring off-duty police officers, if that is an option in your community. You get guards with better training, often with more experience, especially with emergency situations. They also know the local problem folks better and may recognize someone before trouble starts. Usually, hiring off-duty police is more expensive than the usual security guards, so that can be a drawback on thin budgets. Security is important, however, and no library can meet its mission if the staff and patrons don't feel safe.

22

All This Talk about Stress Is Stressing Me Out!

Have you ever gone to work with a severe headache? Maybe worried about a sick child at home? On days like these, the little bumps in the road at work become potholes the size of Montana. Our ability to cope is reduced, and we have a low tolerance for any kind of disagreement. There's little chance that we are prepared to make any extra effort when there's a difficult situation. It's one of those "don't cross me today" days.

For many of us, we will grudgingly admit that we have those kinds of days once in a while. But other people seem to have more bad days at work than good days. They're too serious, stressed out all the time. You've seen the signs—overadhering to the rules, paying attention to details but missing the big picture, being short with patrons and coworkers, complaining about everything, and so forth. Most people didn't start in the library world this way. It was a slow evolution, occurring in spurts over the years.

This condition is often the result of a life out of balance. This can easily happen when your job becomes your life. Just like the change in temperament, this imbalance happened gradually. Over years, the percentage of your time and energy devoted to your job has slowly grown, pushing other priorities to the back burner or completely off the stove. Work should be important, of course, but it's just one part of our existence. Work is what we do, not who we are. That can be hard to remember because our culture puts a huge emphasis on what we do for a living. Our titles give us prestige and social status. Respected titles are automatic admission to elite social circles. Our job occupies forty to sixty hours per week, much more if you add travel time, getting ready, time spent thinking about work, and so forth. All of the time spent and social focus on career make it easy to slip into accepting the job as a definition of the person.

So why is this discussion in a book on dealing with difficult people? Because the first step to dealing with any difficult situation is self-control. If your life is out of balance, self-control is almost impossible. Anything can knock you for a loop. It's like speeding down a brick street in a car with no shock absorbers. When we are in a bad mood, when our life is out of balance, we are much more likely to have unpleasant encounters with patrons, situations where both sides leave unhappy. We should look for ways to prevent problems and approaching every day in a positive frame of mind is a good start.

So what about you? Is stress weakening your ability to stay positive? Do you think your life is out of balance? Does your job take up a disproportionate amount of your time? Try this quiz and see where you come out.

1. Do you get emotional about job issues?
2. Do you stay upset about job issues for more than one day?
3. Are most of your friends (the people you do things with) coworkers?
4. Do you dream about work?
5. Do you talk about work and coworkers frequently to family and friends?
6. Have you ever accumulated more vacation time than you are allowed to, causing you to lose that time?
7. Is it hard for you to leave work at your scheduled time?
8. Are you frequently at work early?
9. Do you often think about work when you are away from the library?
10. Do you have very limited activities outside of work?

Most of us will have to answer yes to a few of these questions during extremely busy times, like in a levy campaign. If, however, you can answer yes to several of these at any given time, you need to do some soul searching. You need to think about the role of work in your life and how to keep it in its proper place.

Focusing too much on work gives a narrow view of the world, where we see everything going on inside the library as the most important activity on the planet. Ironically, this view is likely to damage our performance at work. We're more likely to struggle with everyone because we are overburdened with the significance of our work. That attitude leads to overzealous enforcement of rules and unnecessary confrontations with customers. It's hard to see when to back off and let something minor slide.

To regain some balance between work and nonwork, the first step is to broaden your perspective. Here are a few possible approaches to help accomplish that.

Volunteer some of your free time to help others
Nothing does more to broaden your view than being a part of a larger effort to help improve the world. Volunteer to tutor adults who want to learn to read, help at the Special Olympics, assist a local theater group, deliver meals to the elderly, or find your niche somewhere. If you are stuck for ideas, call your United Way and see if they can give you ideas. Once you are involved in a meaningful, helping activity, you can look at that annoying patron as just one person you have to put up with, not anything more.

Never lose vacation time
If you have time off coming to you—take it! I bet the president does, and you should too.

Make an effort to leave work on time
If you are one of those people who work too much, start cutting back. There may be crunch times when extra hours are required, but those should be the exceptions, not the rule. If you find this hard to do, start keeping a list of what time you leave every day, and make a goal to reduce your work time by an hour or two every week until you are at a level similar to most of your coworkers. This may mean you will have to decide what is really important and what you can drop or delegate, but those choices must be made. You should find you are working more efficiently after a few months.

Put work out of your mind when you leave the library
It doesn't do any good to work fewer hours but still spend as many worrying. When you walk out for the day, remember that you can deal with those unfinished tasks tomorrow, but now it's your time and you can enjoy yourself. If you have trouble doing this, just before you leave, write a to-do list.

Put a star by the top priority for the day. Now you know what you have to accomplish, so forget it until you walk in tomorrow. Remember, the library rents you, they don't own you.

Cultivate connections outside work

Associate with people who have other interests besides the library. Join clubs unrelated to work, take part in church and community activities, go on organized trips, and so forth. If you are around library people all the time, it's too easy to think and talk about work in your time off.

The real asset of the library is its people. Library employees are extremely dedicated to their library and their work, no matter what their job title is. Libraries need that loyalty to prosper, but they also need a healthy, energetic staff. Avoiding burnout is as important to libraries as it is to individuals who work there. So, by keeping yourself healthy and balanced, you are keeping your library strong.

Stressbusters Advice

I Wanna Play in the Mud

My job's too serious
It's making me delirious
I wanna play in the mud.

I'm going to some backyard
After it's rained real hard
I wanna play in the mud.

I'll drag this tie through it
Climb up and dive right into it
I wanna play in the mud.

Gonna leave the city
Where life's not pretty
So I can play in the mud.

Gonna squish my toes in it
Gonna see what grows in it
I wanna play in the mud.

I'll get real dirty
But it won't hurt me
When I get to play in the mud.

My friends can't cope
Trying anything from shrinks to dope
But I'll just play in the mud.

Dirt's at its best
When it's all wet
And we can all play in the mud.

—Mark Willis

23

Memo to the Boss

Memo

TO: The Director and Board of Trustees

FROM: Your Loyal Staff, indirectly

In Shakespeare's *Henry V*, the king disguised himself the evening before a big battle and walked among his soldiers to gauge their mood. It worked for Henry, but it's not likely you will cloak yourself to find out what your troops think (it would probably violate some kind of labor rule anyway), so I'm going to let you know what they say:

> "I wish I had it as easy as the director. She's got nothing to worry about."

> "We got all these new rules. They don't even know what it's like out here on the front lines."

> "Why try to enforce any rule? The director just overrules me anyway."

"Must be nice to spend all day in an office and in meetings. He
never has to deal with all these weirdos and creeps."

"When are we going to hire guards?"

"When are we ever going to hire some good guards?"

"Every day I think it gets more dangerous in here."

"It sure would be nice if administration took our concerns seriously. One day something terrible will happen, and it will be
too late then."

"I need a raise!"

I have talked to frontline staff from around the nation, and there is a
strong consensus that dealing with our patrons is more difficult than ever
before. That opinion seems to be shared by those with five years' as well as
thirty-five years' experience. Staff feel that patrons are more demanding.
They want everything right now. If we can't meet their requests, there is no
hesitation about getting rude, abusive, and even threatening. Basic polite-
ness stills exists but is getting harder to find.

Library staff are also having to deal with more difficult situations than
years ago. Kids have less respect and either ignore a request to quiet down
or respond with contempt. Parents seem more likely to mistreat their children, leaving staff wondering what, if anything, they should do. There are
more homeless people, many with drug-abuse and mental-illness histories.
Drug deals are not rare in some libraries, and no one wants to even con-
template what goes on in some of our rest rooms.

The possibility of violence is on everyone's mind. Almost anyone is free
to come into our library and hang out. If we try to enforce a rule, who
knows whether this will be the time when someone will disagree violently.
Often we have no idea whom we are approaching. We know nothing about
them, and that's scary. We read of shootings in schools, government
offices, and businesses and know we are not immune. Sadly, there have
been tragedies in libraries to confirm that this is not a hypothetical issue.

All of this is going on while staff have to deal daily with the reality of
shrinking budgets and inadequate help on the front lines. These issues are
discussed on a daily basis at circulation desks and reference stations
around the country. And your response, or lack of response, is a significant
part of these discussions.

Odds are, you are aware of these issues and concerned about them. There are severe limits on what you can do. You can't make money appear from nowhere to rent police around the clock. You can't throw out a customer because "he looks scary." You have a thousand things you have to do just to keep the library open and functioning.

How to Improve Morale and Safety

Although you recognize the importance of helping staff deal with difficult situations, budget, administrative concerns, and other details compete for your attention. To make your library safer and your life easier, here's a collection of ideas that will not bust the budget. The amount of your time dedicated to implementing a few of these ideas is reasonable too, especially considering the improved staff morale and library safety that can result. Many of these may be old hat to you, but if you find one or two valuable suggestions, this will be time well spent.

Stay in touch

You may have a pretty good idea of what life is like for your staff but it's best to be sure. The more direct communication and observation, the better your information is. And the larger the library, the harder it is to get this direct information. Here are some tips:

> Work the front desks regularly. Even if it is just a few hours a month at a couple different public service areas, do it regularly. You will have a better understanding of the patrons and see what problems staff are having. Be sure to announce your plan to do this in a positive way, so no one feels you're there to check up on him or her. Let staff know you are there because you are aware of concerns about patron issues and you want to see firsthand. In addition to what you will see, you will increase your rapport with frontline staff, making it easier for them to approach you with concerns and suggestions.

> Encourage complaints. Staff rush to tell you the good news but hide the problems until the lump under the carpet gets too large. It's up to you to change that. How you react to being told about problems determines how often staff share this information. Receive any complaint warmly, even if you don't want to hear it. If the news is bad and you reacted that way, take a few minutes later to tell the person how much you appreciate her effort to inform you.

Send a short note saying "thanks for telling me." Let the person know that things may have gotten much worse without her help. Thank her in front of coworkers. Let her know how the problem was resolved.

Offer an anonymous avenue for expressing concerns. Just like most of us have a suggestion box for patrons, staff need to be able to make their suggestions and concerns known, and not all are willing to do so to your face. No matter how friendly and approachable you are, your position will intimidate some of your staff. Just because they are easily intimidated doesn't mean they don't have concerns and ideas you need to hear. Encourage them to write you a note, use anonymous e-mail, or put their concerns in the patron suggestion box. At staff meetings or in your staff newsletter, regularly review these messages. Summarize the concern and state what you are doing about it. *Be positive!* Even if the concern seems silly to you, it was hard for the staff to express it. Be sure everyone on staff knows you appreciate negative as well as positive feedback. The best way to guarantee continued feedback is to make efforts to address the issues and communicate to staff about the steps you took. Good words are not as encouraging as actions.

Empower staff

Develop and implement policies that empower staff and emphasize security. Giving more authority to staff is actually an important security tool. That's because little problems sometimes become big problems in an instant. For example, the guy who comes in just before closing on April 15 to copy his tax return can become irate and irrational if the copier is broken. All of your staff should know they can make an exception to the normal rules and allow him a few copies on the staff copier in this instance. That accommodation can prevent a patron with a problem from becoming a problem patron. If staff understand that they have some leeway for commonsense application policies, it gives them a chance to find a way to avoid a dangerous situation.

> *Employees should use their own best judgment at all times.*
>
> —The Complete Nordstrom Employee Manual

Tell staff clearly that they have the authority to override policies when it can prevent problems, especially if there is no supervisor available. You may want them to let you know when this happens, but staff must believe that they will not be punished (formally or informally) for this type of action. Staff need to know they have the freedom to make mistakes, especially when trying to give good customer service and prevent problems that could endanger someone.

If you find that a policy is being overridden frequently, reexamine it. A policy should exist only to help things run smoothly. If a policy is having the opposite effect, it probably needs to be revised or eliminated.

Be sure all staff understand they can call the police in an emergency. If two patrons look like they are getting ready to fight, you don't want the person on the desk looking for a supervisor to see about calling the police. Each employee, regardless of position, should be told clearly that he or she can and should call the police in an emergency. An emergency is any situation that looks like there is a possible risk to the health or safety of anyone. After calling the police, the employee should then tell the appropriate supervisor that the police have been called and why. The employee should also know that it is not a problem if the emergency doesn't develop and the police "show up for nothing." Seconds can count in an emergency, and it's better to be safe than sorry. I think most directors would be surprised at the number of staff who are unsure about their authority to call the police. That doubt needs to be completely erased.

Get as much staff input as possible when making policies. Whether you use a formal task-force approach or simply circulate a draft and ask for comments, make every effort to find out what the frontline staff think. They may often be able to tell us what will cause conflict with our patrons. Anything that causes conflict increases the odds of confrontation and even violence. There are times when administration will revise a policy at the request of a few patrons. This well-intentioned change can have a negative impact on other patrons, often representing the silent majority. Following is an example:

Patrons had been asking for an increase in the two-day loan period for videos for quite some time. Because the supply seemed adequate, this responsive library made the change, allowing a week loan and following the same circulation policies of surrounding libraries. The response overwhelmed the system, and shelves were emptied of videos. Patrons yelled at staff and management to fix this stupid mistake. After weathering the storm for a while, it became obvious that this new policy was a complete flop and threatened our very existence (video patrons can make you feel that way!). A revised policy was announced with big signs, complete with an apology. Staff who work with the public were not surprised at the fallout. They could have warned us, if only they had been properly consulted.

Don't allow abuse of staff

Our increased emphasis on customer service is great but sometimes it leads to confusion: "If the customer is always right, I guess I just have to take it when the patron calls me an ignorant loser." I met staff who tolerated much worse operating under the assumption they had to put up with it in the name of customer service. Most directors and trustees would never want staff to feel that way, but that fact must be clearly communicated. Tell them, "You do not have to tolerate abusive language or treatment. Anyone who uses abusive language or is abusive to staff or patrons is warned once, then removed from the library if it happens again." The staff is willing to accept some rudeness as part of the job. Abuse is the sort of treatment that keeps you awake at night, dreading the next day. It should not be part of anyone's work, and the administration's support is the key to stopping it.

Establish ongoing training

Training is more than handing out a manual. Our staff have lots of skills, but the public today can test anyone's abilities. A regular program of classes on the people problems can give your employees new ideas and more confidence in facing their challenges.

Ask what training is needed. A survey is the quickest, easiest way to find out. Distribute an anonymous questionnaire inquiring about particular concerns, with patrons as well as new technology and other issues. Get as much specific information as possible and be open to any ideas.

Help is out there. Once needs are identified, it isn't too hard to find someone to do your training. Many medium-sized and large companies have full-time trainers who specialize in customer-service issues. It's likely you can get a workshop provided for a reasonable price, possibly even donated. There are also individual consultants specializing in customer service issues today. The Chamber of Commerce and local college are good starting points in locating a presenter. Specialized needs can often be met through community resources, too. If the homeless population is a concern identified on the survey, bring in someone from a homeless support organization. Counseling agencies, children's services, mental health programs, hospitals, police, and United Way organizations are often helpful and affordable. Small libraries should consider working with neighboring libraries to share costs and planning efforts.

Computers can help. Encourage staff to join library discussion groups on the Internet where these ideas are discussed. It's like attending a conference everyday, without the mileage expenses.

Train on policies. Sending out a memo is easy, but it's not the most effective way to do training. Every new employee should get a personal, formal orientation to the policies for dealing with patron problems. Whenever new rules are developed, all staff should receive small-group instruction that explains the purpose behind the rules, how to apply the rules, when staff can make exceptions, how to enforce the rules and where to send a patron who disagrees with the rules. Give specific examples of what to say to customers about the rules, which helps to ensure a consistent message and gives the staff some ideas.

Situation of the Day

Here's a case study. The board voted to prohibit rollerblades in the library. What now?

The Easy Way

A memo stating this rule is sent to all staff, who are told they may eject anyone who violates the rule. Colorful signs are affixed to the doors and sprinkled around the building. Problem solved? Maybe not.

The Better Way

The rule is passed by the board, and it is agreed that the rule will not take place until staff are trained and ready to enforce it. There is a monthly staff meeting already scheduled for a week after the board meeting, so this is the best training opportunity. The director and several staff members who will have to enforce the rule sit down and work out a one-page training outline. The results are handed out before the meeting, and the staff will also present it at the meeting. Here's a sample:

Memo

TO: All Staff

FROM: M. Dewey, Director

NEW RULE PROHIBITS ROLLERBLADES IN LIBRARY

The board of trustees yesterday unanimously passed a new policy prohibiting the wearing of rollerblades inside the library. The rules will go into effect after our staff meeting next week. We have had growing problems with this for the last year, and many staff suggested this rule. After checking with our legal staff, it was agreed that this is the best way to go. Your help is needed in enforcing this. Here are guidelines to help you when enforcing this rule. Special thanks to Cherie and Moira in the Circulation Department for their assistance in developing these guidelines!

Q. What do I do when a customer asks, "Why can't I wear my rollerblades in the library anymore?"

A. Tell them this: "We had allowed it for a long time, but lately there have been a number of problems. One person fell and almost knocked down an elderly patron. The rollerblades damage the floor, and we have had complaints about the noise. Because of this, the board passed a rule against them. I'm sorry about the inconvenience."

Q. What do we do when someone ignores the signs and rolls on in?

A. Approach the customer and state that we have a rule prohibiting rollerblades. Explain the reasons and be polite. If the patron is returning materials, offer to take care of that and suggest the outside book drop next time. If the person refuses to comply, explain that this is an important safety issue and failure to follow the rule can mean removal from the library. If the patron continues, follow our usual procedure for removing an unruly customer, including calling the police if necessary.

Q. Are there ever exceptions?

A. It may occasionally make sense to let a patron complete a quick transaction, especially the first month or so, while the rule is new. For example, if someone rolls in the front entrance and over to the circulation desk, explain the rule. If the patron doesn't have shoes to wear but just needs to renew a book, take care of that. Be sure the patron knows the rule, and offer to give him or her a copy of our rules, which have been updated to include this one.

Q. If the patron doesn't have shoes to change into, can he or she use the library in sock feet?

A. No, that's also a safety concern and prohibited by the Board of Health. We would just be exchanging one safety problem for another.

Q. What options can we offer patrons who can't come in because they only wore rollerblades?

A. There are a few things we can do. Offer to hold items or send them to another branch. If they are here to look up information, suggest telephone reference or the "Internet from Home" service if they have a connection. If they have a simple reference question, offer to write it down and pass it to the reference department. Get names and phone numbers so we can call them back.

Q. Who can patrons talk to if they wish to complain about this rule?

A. Because it has been approved by the board, only the board can change it. Direct those who wish to discuss it to the director or invite them to attend the next regularly scheduled board meeting. As with any complaint, any supervisor can talk to the patron who wants to talk now and the director is unavailable.

It always takes some time for the public to get accustomed to a change like this, so please be patient. We will discuss how it's going at next month's staff meeting. If you have questions or problems with this new rule, please let me know immediately. Thanks!

The training at the staff meeting can be a simple, five-minute presentation. Give the staff a little background; then, have a few staff members act out a couple of examples. Sometimes, having the actor portraying the staff member saying everything wrong gives the presentation some humor while also making a point. Ask for questions and carefully scan the room for quizzical looks or troubled expressions, both of which suggest some kind of doubts.

The "Better Way" is a little more work than the "Easy Way," but it may save lots of time in the long run and also gives the staff the guidance needed to do their jobs properly. We wouldn't bring in a new computer system and turn staff loose on it without training. Patron issues deserve as much attention.

Train on Security and Safety

Are your staff trained as well as they need to be? If so, they should all be able to give the correct answer to questions such as these:

Who is authorized to call the police in an emergency?

What do you do if you encounter an abusive patron?

What constitutes *abuse*?

What exactly do all of our "Rules of Behavior" mean?

Who's responsible for enforcing each rule?

When can staff make an exception to a rule?

What do you do if a six-year-old is still here at closing time?

How do you handle a fight between patrons?

What do you do about a customer who has a severe body odor?

What do you do if you feel a rule needs to be changed because it is causing more problems than it is preventing?

If you get different answers to these questions from different staff members, training may be needed.

Make a commitment to security

I know that the thought of making a commitment to security sent dollar signs flying around in your head, but this is not just a money issue. Some security options are affordable. Other times, it may be a matter of deciding that a larger portion of the budget will have to be spent on security. Many other companies are deciding that today, and we may not be able to avoid that decision in the library world. Our exposure is greater than many places because we allow virtually anyone in our building.

There are some options that are not big-ticket items. The first step is to work with your local police. Most departments offer free crime-prevention analysis, meaning an inspection of your building and, often, a discussion of your policies and problems. It's a good free starting point. There are other specific suggestions in chapter 21.

The first step for the leadership of the library is to decide that the safety of the staff and patrons is worth time and money. That means taking every concern seriously and looking for effective remedies.

Before we conclude this chapter, I want to pass on a concluding message from frontline staff everywhere. You may find this hard to believe, but there is a surprising amount of actual fear in many libraries. Staff have seen too many cases of random violence in the news, and many can pick out a patron who they think may be capable of hurting staff and patrons. I bet that most frontline staff have discussed among themselves at least one candidate for "going postal." It's that much a part of life in a public library. It's a sad commentary on the world today, but it's one we have to accept.

Your staff are looking to you for leadership and support in facing these patron problems. They will judge you both by your words and your actions. If you expect *them* to take security seriously, show them *you* take it seriously. Your staff realize they have to deal with these challenges, and they are ready. They are waiting for you to get them started.

24

Wrapping Up

Solving people problems is 1 percent inspiration and
99 percent communication.

The staff in a public library will always face a challenge from the people we serve. When you combine all ages, races, and social groups in one building and ask them to play nicely together, you can't count on complete cooperation. There will be times when we have to send a few to time-out. Some won't go willingly. Although most of our guests are interested in finding information or just a good read, these few noncooperators will test us.

We have learned a few simple, basic steps toward meeting these tests. If we follow these steps, we will be successful most of the time with any difficult-people situation. Time to review these steps:

1. Understand how to deal with difficult situations when they arise. Remember that we can control ourselves and control the situation, but we can't control another person.

> *Take a deep breath and a pause.* Before taking off into tough territory, collect your thoughts. Know what you want to say before you speak.

> *Stay calm.* It's fine to feel a little nervous, especially in a confrontational situation, but keep your composure and avoid emotional

responses. If this specific instance is something you can't handle, get help.

Remember, safety first. Don't end up alone with an angry or irrational patron. Alert others and be prepared to call the police.

Share information and use teamwork. If you know a particular patron is likely to cause problems, get the staff involved and make a plan on how to head the patron off at the pass.

2. Be prepared. We know many of the types of situations we will encounter. We can prepare by writing effective policies and training staff.

Write effective policies. Clear, direct guidelines tell the patrons what to expect and let the staff know what to enforce. Rules must be easily understood by all and revisited regularly to keep them current. These policies should be written with the assistance of the frontline staff who will have to deal with them. All rules should have legal review and be approved by the overseeing body (board of trustees, city commission, etc.).

Train staff. Everyone who may have to work with policies must understand them, why they exist, and how patrons can complain about them (name of supervisors, address for board of trustees, etc.). Staff must know which complaints are referred to which supervisors and how a patron can address the library's governing board. Staff must know their enforcement roles. They need to be able to successfully answer, "What would I do if I saw someone breaking rule number 3?" Staff also must have some leeway on enforcing rules, meaning they can modify or override a rule any time it will help the library operate more efficiently. Staff must be told that they have this authority and be encouraged to use it. They will only feel encouraged as long as management supports the decisions made by staff.

3. Use good communication skills. Most of our difficult situations with patrons can be either avoided or at least minimized by learning and using good communications skills. The good news is that these skills can be learned, practiced, and improved. Start with a recognition of their importance; then, follow with a decision to work toward constant improvement.

Listening is the key. The most overlooked skill in conversation is listening to the other person. It's beyond the physical act of hearing and involves thinking about what the other person means. A good listener will give the speaker plenty of time to state the message and ask questions to clarify any vague points. Paying attention to nonverbal messages such as body language, facial expressions, and tone of voice adds meaning to the words. Much of listening involves giving up our perceptions and avoiding assumptions or mental arguments with the speaker. We need to eliminate barriers to understanding, open ourselves up to hearing things we may not want to hear, and make the effort to grasp the speaker's message. Forget the popular image of the slickster who can fast talk his way out of any jam—the better approach is to listen your way out of trouble.

Speak clearly. Simple and direct words work better than those vocabulary-builder words. Take a moment to think about the message you want to send before speaking. Help the other person listen by avoiding jargon and information overload. Stick to one point at a time, and be sure the patron understands fully before going forward.

Work to continually improve your communication skills. After any challenging interaction, reflect on what you heard and said. What would you have done differently? Was there one point where the conversation went wrong? Ask coworkers if they thought there was some different way to handle the situation. Observe others as they communicate, and learn from their successes and failures (always better than learning from your own failures!). Constantly search for ways to build your communications skills.

All of these techniques will help only if we keep ourselves in the proper frame of mind. If we walk into work with too much stress, there's no way we can expect to control a difficult encounter. We won't stay calm, we won't listen objectively, and we won't speak in a positive tone of voice. It's likely we will only succeed in fanning the flames. A positive attitude and an understanding that this is probably not going to lead to the end of the world give the right perspective. Keep your sense of humor handy, and apply it often.

Now that you've struggled through every word of this book, we can boil it down to this:

1. Stay calm.
2. Listen!
3. Treat everyone with respect.
4. Have a plan to deal with frequent problems.
5. Use your best judgment.
6. Have fun!

Good luck!

APPENDIXES

1. An Overview of Mental Illnesses

Overview of Mental Illnesses

Usually staff training doesn't go into much detail on types of mentally ill patrons we may encounter on the job. It is worthwhile to have a little general information about these types and how we can deal with them. While we aren't hired to be therapists, recognizing the signs of mental illness can help us control a difficult situation. If your library finds itself dealing with people with mental illnesses, look into arranging a training session with a community health program to learn more about these illnesses and the resources in your community.

Depression is one of the most common types of mental illnesses but one of the most misunderstood. Everyone will experience some down days, sadness, and unhappiness. This is different from the clinical depression that is disabling to millions of Americans. Comparing the blues we all feel to clinical depression is like comparing a standard headache to a migraine. While some of the symptoms are similar, there's a huge difference in duration, cause, impact, and severity.

Besides the sadness that we think of with depression, there are often feelings of lethargy, apathy, lack of self-worth, difficulty in concentrating, and fatigue. Inability to sleep is common, but sleep may also become a refuge, and a clinically depressed person may sleep long hours as an escape. Thoughts of death and suicide are not uncommon. As a result of these symptoms, someone suffering from clinical depression may be unable to accomplish the smallest of life's tasks.

Everyday depression usually arises from a specific cause—death of a loved one, severe illness, family problems, financial setbacks, etc. Clinical depression sometimes has its roots in an identifiable cause but often seems to come out of nowhere. People who deal with depression throughout their life may have years where they are relatively symptom free, followed by years of serious depression. The inability to explain one's depression can be as devastating as the depression itself.

This type of depression can affect any age, from a young child to a senior citizen. Women are much more likely than men to be diagnosed with clinical depression. The disease seems to run in families. It is also often associated with alcoholism and substance abuse. Medication and therapy can often successfully treat depression, but many people either don't seek treatment or give up too easily.

In the library—A patron going through a clinical depression is unlikely to cause a disturbance in the library. On the other hand, if a depressed person has a problem, such as late materials, dealing with it can be overwhelming. It is easier to walk away from the problem. If there is an issue with someone who you think is severely depressed, look for ways to remove barriers to cooperation. Smooth the path as much as possible. For example, instead of suggesting the patron contact the director on an issue, you may want to offer to have the director send a letter explaining the issue. A depressed person is unlikely to make the effort to call the director or come in and complain.

Our usual fines and penalties are not significant. The depression is bigger than any consequence the library can impose. Look for easy ways for the patron to cooperate.

Schizophrenia is often connected to some of the most bizarre behaviors we see. Talking to an imaginary person, hearing things, delusions, hallucinations, inappropriate responses, and distorted thinking can all be symptoms. Partly because of these severe symptoms, the person is often isolated and avoids most social contact. Keeping a regular job with uncontrolled symptoms is almost impossible. The isolation and difficulty in holding a job mean it is not uncommon for someone with this disorder to find himself hanging out in a public library. Schizophrenia is sometimes confused with split personality, which is a totally separate condition.

The disease usually starts showing up in adolescence or the early twenties; the first occurrence almost never happens after forty It affects males and females equally, although it shows up earlier in men. Like cancer, schizophrenia is not one disease but an umbrella for a variety of related conditions and may affect as many as two million Americans. The causes are unclear, but it is most likely a brain disorder, like Parkinson's disease. Children are at a greater risk of someday having schizophrenia if one parent has it and at an even greater risk if both parents do. Treatment includes hospitalization and medication. Advances in treatment are improving the lives of many people suffering from this condition. A major challenge is preventing the person from discontinuing the medication and therapy needed to control symptoms.

In the library one of the biggest problems that affect us is when the person doesn't take the medication. This is compounded when the person lacks family or other support systems. As we discussed, there is no use in trying to argue the patron out of his delusions. Family, friends, and medical professionals can't, so there's no use in us trying. While you certainly don't want to play into any distorted, imagined situations, you do have to accept that they are real to the person. You may need to acknowledge what the person is experiencing while still attempting to handle the situation. "I understand that you are hearing voices and that's disturbing you. However, you are also making too much noise and that's causing a problem for people trying to study. Is there someone I can call to help you get home?" The best strategy in dealing with someone in a schizophrenic episode is to do the minimum. In other words, end the situation as quickly as possible. If someone is hearing voices and getting upset, that's not the time to explain the video-lending policy. Be polite, firm, and quickly try to wrap up only essential business.

Anxiety, like depression, is something we all experience. Also similar to depression, anxiety can be a sign of mental illness when it is acute, irrational, and ongoing. Symptoms include trembling, hot flashes or cold chills, tenseness, irritability, shortness of breath, and a fear of going completely out of control.

The exact causes of anxiety disorders are not known, but there are indications that genetic factors may play a role. It may start in childhood but not show up strongly until a person reaches her twenties, and it is more common in women than men.

A paralyzing bout of anxiety is called a *panic attack*. Some of the symptoms are similar to general anxiety, but there is an increased, irrational fear of dying, rapid heartbeat, and a feeling of detachment or unreality. Some estimates say that more than three million Americans have suffered from full-blown panic attacks and more than twice that number have experienced some of the symptoms of a panic attack.

Another related condition is *phobia*, an irrational fear of an object or situation. Common examples include fear of flying, going out in public, elevators, etc. All of us have fears, but when one of our fears severely restricts our ability to function, we may have crossed over to a phobia.

Obsessive-compulsive disorders are also connected to anxiety. An obsessive person may be consumed with a fear of germs, fire, leaving the house unlocked, etc. In order to deal with this obsessive fear, the person may develop a compulsive behavior. For example, a person obsessed with germs may wash his hands hundreds of times a day and take irrational steps to avoid coming into contact with germs (such as wearing gloves, spraying a telephone receiver with disinfectant, etc.).

Post-traumatic stress syndrome is another anxiety-related disorder. We most often think of this with military veterans, but it can also occur in anyone who has endured a life-threatening event, such as a car crash, tornado, or physical abuse. In some cases, anything that reminds the person of this trauma can cause flashbacks and extreme anxiety. For example, someone who lived through a destructive storm may become anxious when the weather conditions are similar to the severe storm.

All of these varieties of anxiety can generally be successfully treated using a combination of methods. Training in relaxation techniques, biofeedback, meditation, etc. can help with anxiety. Counseling and medication may also be used. For some phobias and obsessions, additional treatments can include gradual, supervised exposure to the source of fear, in combination with therapy and medication. While the success rate for these various disorders related to anxiety is good, many people go untreated because the condition is not properly diagnosed. Treatment can be fairly brief in some cases, lifelong in more severe situations.

Since these various anxiety disorders are not uncommon, we could easily find ourselves dealing with patrons suffering from these illnesses. Recognizing that a stressed patron may be showing unusual signs of nervousness is the first step. This nervousness could be a sign of an anxiety disorder.

In most cases we need only exercise our very best people skills and a little extra patience and sensitivity. For example, if a patron is showing signs of anxiety, we need to be sure not to rush her or show any signs that we are feeling rushed. Any extra pressure will just make the anxiety worse for the patron and make our job more difficult. A smile and kind words such as "Take your time; I'm in no hurry" can go a long way. Even if we are simply dealing with an overly stressed patron, this kind of service never hurts.

If you are faced with a patron who seems to be having a panic attack, you will need to be extremely calm. Part of the distress of a panic attack comes from a fear of fear, a belief that things may spiral out of control. Use a calm, reassuring tone of voice and let the person know that everything will be okay. Ask what you can do to help her. This way you are giving the patron some control and also something else to think about other than the cause of the panic. Offer to call an ambulance or someone whom the patron may want to come and help. If you don't know the patron's name, ask and give your name. It is easier to help if you can use names. Offer to find a quiet place to sit away from the public. While you don't want to hover over her, you also should be sure not to leave her alone for long. If the person is having trouble breathing or breathing rapidly, you may want to encourage slow, deep breaths. It is a good idea to have a glass of water handy, as some people may have medicine to take. Remember, you don't have to play therapist; simply give some basic support and assistance and be prepared to call for medical help if a panic attack continues too long.

Suicide—this isn't really a mental illness, but it's a difficult situation that you may encounter. Knowing a little more can help. For most people who consider suicide, it is not death they seek but an escape from the pain they feel. Out of desperation, death seems to become the only option.

Suicide affects all ages and groups. While teen suicide has grown and become more recognized lately, suicide in the elderly is also growing. Women are more likely to attempt suicide, but men are more likely to actually complete the act, partially because men are much more likely to use a gun. People who talk about suicide are often likely to attempt it.

There are usually telltale clues of someone considering suicide. These include talking about death, giving away important personal possessions, wrapping up personal and professional business, disassociating with people, or fixating on a certain song or poem. Often, there is a twenty-four-to-forty-eight-hour period when the person seems happier and "like his old self." This is often a time when the person has decided to commit suicide and is just waiting for the right opportunity, such as a time when no one is at home. Not all of these signs are found in all cases but at least some are usually found.

In the library if you hear someone talking about wanting to "end it all," take it seriously. You can ask, "Are you thinking about killing yourself?" If you have reason to suspect the person is considering suicide, contact your suicide prevention center or the police. As library staff, we do not have to try to talk someone out of suicide, but we should be willing to summon help in the same way we would if a patron was exhibiting signs of a heart attack.

Summary

It helps to understand mental illness. Bringing in a local professional for staff training can be helpful. As always, treat the person with respect, stay calm, and do not touch a person who is upset, mentally ill or not.

The samples following represent a range of approaches to library issues. Many will reinforce concepts discussed in the book; some will add information and others will be in conflict. They are here to offer you several points of view for consideration. The Internet has numerous other examples and your state library association may be helpful in finding even more.

Remember, the policies which work in one library may not work in your library. Laws are different in various states and cities so always be sure to check your proposed rules with your local legal authorities. Don't assume that a rule is legal because you know it's in place in another library. It could have recently been overruled or the law in your community may be different.

I want to thank all the libraries that allowed me to use their policies as samples. These are good starting points but your final policy must be a result of *your* process, addressing *your* specific needs and following the laws of *your* community.

2. Sample Internet Policies

INTERNET POLICIES

Local Area Network Policy and Network Usage Guidelines

Local Area Network Policy

The Westerville Public Library, through the development of the Library Channel, provides access to the Internet and other electronic services to further our mission of selecting informational and educational resources of value to our community. These services are offered in conformity with the Library Bill of Rights, the Freedom to Read policy, and the Freedom to View policy. The Internet and the Greater Columbus Free-Net contain many different kinds of material, some of which may be deemed to be of a controversial or offensive nature. In offering Internet and Free-Net access, the library staff cannot control nor assume total responsibility for access points reached,

the content of interactive communication such as e-mail and news-groups,

the validity of information,

or accessibility due to technical difficulties or Internet reliability.

Inappropriate Use

In order to comply with contemporary community standards regarding obscenity as defined in 2907.01 of the Ohio Revised Code, the library deems as inappropriate the following uses:

Display of sexually explicit graphics

Display or transmission of profane, abusive or threatening language

In addition, the following practices are deemed inappropriate:

Use for informal conversations, such as chat groups.

Unauthorized copying of copyright-protected materials.

Violating any local, state, or federal statute.

Parental Responsibility

Parents must share with the library the responsibility for their children's use of the Internet and the Free-Net in the library. Access to material that is considered harmful to juveniles as described in the "Obscenity" section of the Ohio Revised Code 2907.31 will not be permitted through the Library Channel because those materials do not support the mission of the library. Free copies of Child Safety on the Information Highway are available in each department.

Procedure for Filing a Concern

Those persons having a concern about access to the Internet and the Greater Columbus Free-Net should ask at the Circulation Desk for the Statement of Concern Request. The completed statement should be returned to the Circulation Desk for processing.

GUIDELINES FOR LOCAL AREA NETWORK USE

By using the Westerville Public Library's network, customers agree to the following:

These workstations are part of the library's Local Area Network (LAN). Each workstation in the network is set up to run pre-installed library software only.

Do not attempt to run your own software, customize files, or change configurations.

Do not turn off the computer or reboot the system. Ask a library staff member for assistance.

When finished, please close the application you have used and return to the main menu.

Security

Deliberate altering of any files or modifying the configuration of any PC or peripherals is considered a violation of computer system security and will result in the loss of library computer privileges, with possible legal ramifications.

Destruction or damage of equipment due to willful misuse will result in legal action.

Willful removal of any part of the PC will be considered theft and will result in legal action.

Staff Assistance

Staff provide assistance, as time and knowledge permit.

Scheduled demonstrations are offered periodically. Please see a reference librarian to register.

Circulating and Reference books and manuals for self-instruction are available. Please ask a librarian.

Time Limits

There is a thirty-minute limit when others are waiting.

Workstations not in use will be logged off five minutes before closing.

Printing

Prints at each workstation are free.

Do not refill paper trays. Ask a library staff member for assistance.

Downloading

Downloading and file transfer protocol (FTP) are not available.

Disk drives have been disabled for security reasons.

E-mail

The library does not offer e-mail accounts.

E-mail accounts are available through the Greater Columbus Free-Net. These accounts may be accessed on the LAN.

Applications are available at the bulletin board by the Circulation Desk.

Newsgroups

The library's Internet connection does not provide access to newsgroups.

Newsgroups are accessible through the Greater Columbus Free-Net, which is available on the LAN.

Customers violating any usage guideline will be asked to stop. If the violation continues, the customers will forfeit the right to use the computers at the Westerville Public Library.

From Westerville, Ohio, Public Library. Used with permission.

Internet Access Policy

The West Orange Public Library strives to be the gateway to the global network of recorded thought and information. We are committed to providing superior services to our diverse communities, as well as employing state-of-the-art technology to improve access to global resources. As part of our mission to meet informational, educational, and recreational needs of our public, the Library makes available free access to the Internet.

The Library endorses the American Library Association Library Bill of Rights. All Library users are provided equal access to resources available on the Internet.

The Library does not endorse the viewpoints or vouch for the accuracy, timeliness, content, or authenticity of materials accessed via the Internet. It is left to each user to determine what material is appropriate. Parents or guardians of minors using the Internet are responsible for providing guidance to the children under their care.

Users have the right of confidentiality in all their activities with resources and services provided by the Library. The Library supports the user's right to privacy, however, users are advised that because security is technically difficult to achieve, electronic communications and files could become public.

The Library reserves the right to terminate an Internet session at any time.

Approved by the Board of Trustees 3/21/96.

From West Orange, New Jersey, Public Library. Used with permission.

Internet Access at the
Boston Public Library

The Boston Public Library endeavors to develop collections, resources, and services that meet the cultural, informational, recreational, and educational needs of the diverse, multicultural community it serves. It is within this context that the Boston Public Library offers access to the Internet.

The Internet is a global electronic network. Resources available on the Internet supplement and complement the collections of the Boston Public Library. All Internet resources accessible through the Library are provided equally to all library users. The Boston Public Library does not monitor and has no control over the information accessed through the Internet, and cannot be held responsible for its content. The Internet and its available resources may contain material of a controversial nature. The Boston Public Library neither censors access to materials nor protects users from information they may find offensive. Library users access the Internet at their own discretion and are responsible for any access points they reach.

The Boston Public Library provides computers with filtering software to limit children's exposure to some Web sites. The software blocks some specific sites that could be offensive to some users. Filtering software may not block all material users might find offensive. Parents may wish to supervise their children's Internet sessions. Parents may give their children approval to use unfiltered computers.

Library staff cannot control the availability of information links which often change rapidly and unpredictably. Not all sources on the Internet provide accurate, complete or current information. Users need to be good information consumers, questioning the validity of the information.

Users should always be good citizens of the electronic community of the Internet. Users should abide by the rules and procedures of the library as well as those of remote systems. The user may not use the Internet for any illegal activity or place any material on the Internet related to any illegal activity. It is the responsibility of the user to respect copyright laws and licensing agreements and assume responsibility for payment of fees for any fee-based service. Use of the Internet is a privilege, not a right. Inappropriate use will result in a cancellation of this privilege.

Library staff cannot provide in-depth training on Internet operations or personal computer skills. Staff may, however, be able to offer searching suggestions and answer questions.

Guidelines for Access to the Internet at the Boston Public Library

By using a public Internet workstation at the Boston Public Library you agree to the following guidelines:

Time limits:

You must sign in with Library staff before using the Internet computer; a valid library card is necessary for computer use.

There are time limits on computer use per day; the limit may vary according to location, and level of demand.

Downloading:

You may download to a pre-formatted disk.

You must provide your own disks.

The library is not responsible for any loss or damage to personal disks when downloading.

E-Mail:

The library does not offer electronic mail accounts.

You may download your e-mail if you know the Internet address of your private account.

YOU MAY NOT:

- Use the library's workstations as a staging ground to gain unauthorized access to the library's networks or computer systems or to any other network or computer system.
- Obstruct the work of others by consuming gratuitously large amounts of system resources or by deliberately crashing any library computer system.
- Make any attempt to damage computer equipment or software.
- Make any attempt to alter software configurations in a malicious manner.
- Make any attempt to cause degradation of system performance.

Use any library workstation for illegal or criminal purpose.

Engage in any activity which is deliberately and maliciously offensive, libelous or slanderous.

Represent yourself as another person for purposes of fraud or other illegal activity.

Illegal acts involving library resources may be subject to prosecution by local, state or federal officials.

The Library reserves the right to terminate an Internet session at any time.
5/7/97
BPL Internet Access Policy, July 31, 1997

From Boston Public Library. Used with permission.

Use of
Computer Resources Policy

Use of Computer Resources Generally

The library provides access to computer equipment, programs, databases, and the Internet (collectively, "the computer resources") for informational and educational purposes. All users of the library's computer resources, both staff members and patrons, are expected to use these resources correctly and only for legal and ethical purposes. Computer resources may not be used for the following purposes:

Violation of any applicable federal, state, or local laws, ordinances, rules, or regulations.

Harassment of other persons or parties.

Libel or slander of other persons or parties.

Destruction of or damage to equipment, software, or data belonging to the library or other uses.

Gaining or attempting to gain unauthorized access to any computing, information or communications devices or resources.

Disruption or unauthorized monitoring of electronic communications.

Unauthorized copying of copyright or other protected material.

Violation of computer system security.

Unauthorized use of computer accounts, access codes, or network identification numbers assigned to others.

Use of computer communications facilities in ways that unnecessarily impede the computing activities of others (such as randomly initiating interactive electronic communications or email exchanges, overuse of interactive network utilities, etc.).

Violation of software license agreements.

Violation of network usage policies and regulations.

Violation of another person's or party's privacy.

Any and all other matters which the library, in its sole discretion, and in consideration of the best interests of the public, determines to be an unacceptable purpose.

Internet Access

The library provides Internet access to the public in order to make available a vast array of information resources and to allow members of the public to become familiar with state-of-the-art information technology.

The Internet and its available resources contain a wide variety of material and opinions from varied points of view. In offering Internet access, library staff cannot control access points which often change rapidly and unpredictably. Users are hereby notified that they are responsible for the access points they reach. Parents of minor children must assume responsibility for their children's use of or exposure to the Internet through the library's connection.

The Allen County Public Library assumes no responsibility for any damages, direct or indirect, arising from the use of its World Wide Web server or from its connections to other Internet services.

Use of Internet Workstations

The demand for use of the Library's Internet workstations may exceed the available supply. Therefore, it is necessary to manage Internet access fairly and equitably so that all patrons will have an opportunity to use the resource.

Each agency manager is therefore authorized to employ whatever reasonable methods he or she deems appropriate in order to ensure that access to Internet workstations is available to all patrons who wish to use them. Examples of methods that might be employed include, but are not necessarily limited to:

1. Establishing time limits and using sign-up sheets to reserve time on Internet workstations.

2. Asking a patron to relinquish a workstation when, in the judgment of the staff member on duty, that patron has had a fair opportunity to use the workstation and other patrons are waiting to use it.

3. Asking a patron to relinquish a workstation temporarily when, in the judgment of the staff member on duty, another patron or staff member has a more critical need to use the workstation.

4. Asking a patron to relinquish a workstation when, in the judgment of the staff member on duty, that patron has used a computer resource for any of the above stated unacceptable purposes or has otherwise violated any portion of this policy.

The library does not attempt to restrict access to Internet sites. The library wishes to make the Internet and all computer resources available to anyone who respects the rights and property of others, including the library, and who abides by these policies. While patrons are free to access whatever Internet sites they wish, the library must also be mindful and respectful of the rights of other patrons (particularly children) not to be inadvertently exposed to material and images they (or their parents) may find personally unsuitable. In fact, the library is obligated to comply with federal law regarding the use of computer resources in the prevention of exposure to certain explicit images and material.

Therefore, staff members will request that a patron remove such an image or text from an Internet workstation screen if, in the staff member's judgment, the image or text is displayed in such a way that other patrons, particularly children, are exposed to or cannot reasonably avoid viewing it in the course of carrying out their business in the library.

From Allen County (Ind.) Public Library. Used with permission.

3. Sample Children's Policies

POLICIES ON UNATTENDED CHILDREN AND DISRUPTIVE YOUTH JULY 12

Due to widespread interest and concern over the growing problem of latchkey children in libraries, the Children's Services Department developed the following policies and procedures on Unattended Children and Disruptive Youth. These were adopted by the Board of Library Trustees in November, 1988.

Policy Statement

The staff of the Dayton and Montgomery County Public Library are happy you are visiting with us. We are concerned about the safety of all library users, especially children. We strive to make the library an enjoyable place to visit so that you, your family and friends will want to return many times.

Library staff members cannot, however, supervise children or function as substitute baby-sitters. Parents and responsible persons need to be as careful of their children's safety in the library as they would be in a shopping mall or any other public building. Children can easily wander out the door, into the street or parking lot. They can be injured by swinging doors or by falls from furniture.

The Board of Trustees of the Dayton and Montgomery County Public Library has, therefore, established the following policies for all agencies of the library system.

POLICY ON UNATTENDED CHILDREN

Children under age seven may not be left unattended in the library. Parents and/or responsible persons (age 14 or older) are accountable for their children's behavior and safety while in the library.

POLICY ON DISRUPTIVE YOUTH

Disruptive youth over the age of seven will be asked to leave after two warnings, with notification of parent and/or local authorities. Disruptive behavior is any behavior on library premises which infringes on the rights of others using and/or working in the library.

Established library procedures will be used to implement these policies.

PROCEDURES FOR HANDLING UNATTENDED CHILDREN UNDER AGE 7

Children under the age of seven may not be left unattended in the library. They must be accompanied by a parent or other responsible person at all times. Parents and/or responsible persons are accountable for their children's behavior and safety while in the library.

1. Children left unattended are often frightened and crying and should be comforted by the staff. If it becomes apparent that a child under the age of seven is lost or has been left unattended, a staff member will try to identify and locate the parent or other person responsible for the child by walking through the library with the child or by paging the responsible person. The meeting rooms should also be checked.

2. When the parent/responsible person is located, the staff member will explain the library's policy on unattended children, stressing concern for the child's safety. The parent/responsible person will be given a copy of the policy.

3. If the person responsible is not located in the library, every effort should be made to locate the child's parents by telephone. A staff member will stay with the child while this is being done. If a parent is reached, insist that the child be picked up immediately, explaining the library's policy. (refer to #2 above)

4. If the child's parents have not been located within thirty minutes, or sooner if the library is closing, the librarian (or staff member) in charge will call the police who will then assume responsibility for the child. The librarian (or staff member) in charge, and one other staff member will stay with the child until the proper authorities arrive.

5. Under no circumstances will staff take the child out of the library.

PROCEDURES FOR HANDLING DISRUPTIVE CHILDREN/YOUTH

Children under Age 7:

1. Warn the child verbally that his/her behavior is unacceptable and explain appropriate library behavior.

2. If the behavior continues, a staff member will inform the responsible person of the library's policy and issue a verbal warning.

3. If the disruptive behavior still continues, the responsible person will be asked to take the child out of the library.

4. If the responsible person refuses or cannot control the child's behavior, the family will be asked to leave. If they refuse, the librarian (or staff member) in charge will call police.

5. Under no circumstances should staff appear to be using force with disruptive patrons.

Youth Age 7 to 18:

1. Warn the disruptive patron that his/her behavior is unacceptable. The staff member will explain what the appropriate behavior should be. Tell the patron that this is a verbal warning. (If circumstances warrant, i.e., life-threatening situations, repeat offenders, verbal abuse, etc., go immediately to step 3 listed below.)

2. If the disruptive behavior persists, approach the youth and the responsible person with the same warning as detailed in step 1. If the youth is unattended, give him/her a second warning. State that this is a warning and if the disruptive behavior persists, the youth will be asked to leave the library premises.

3. If the disruptive behavior still persists:
   a) Request that the youth and the responsible person leave the library premises.
   b) If the responsible person cannot be located within the building, the staff will attempt to contact the responsible person by telephone. If the responsible person is located, he/she will be told the youth is being disruptive and they will be reminded of the library policy. They will be told to pick up the youth immediately.
   c) For youth 7 to 14, if the responsible person cannot be located within thirty minutes, and the youth refuses to leave the library, the staff should contact the police. If circumstances warrant, the police may be called sooner.

4. Youth ages 14 to 18 may be asked to leave after the second warning. If the youth refuses to leave, the staff should call the police.

5. Under no circumstances should staff appear to be using force with disruptive patrons.

CLOSING TIME PROCEDURES FOR UNATTENDED CHILDREN, 14 AND UNDER

If a staff member observes an unattended child thirty minutes prior to closing, that staff member will ask the child what his/her provisions are for getting home. If the child seems unsure, the staff member in charge of the agency will call the parents. If closing time arrives and the child is still in the library:

1. An attempt will be made to call the parents. If a parent is contacted, insist that the child be picked up immediately.

2. If a parent cannot be reached, the police department will be contacted, with the request that someone pick up the child as abandoned.

3. The librarian (or staff member) in charge, and one other staff member will remain in the building with the child until parent, guardian, or police officer arrives.

4. A copy of the library policy on unattended children will be handed to the child's parents, or to the child.

5. Under no circumstances shall a staff member take a child out of the building.

CLOSING TIME PROCEDURES FOR UNATTENDED YOUTH OVER AGE 14

If an unattended youth over 14 years old is still in the library at closing time:

1. An attempt will be made to contact the parents by the staff member in charge of the agency. If a parent is contacted, insist that the youth be picked up immediately.

2. If a parent cannot be contacted, the youth should be given the option of waiting outside the library or locked in the foyer (where possible).

For any youth left at the library after closing, the parent's name and address should be obtained and sent to the Director, who will send a letter to the parent stressing that the library and its employees cannot be responsible for youths not picked up at the library at closing.

From Dayton and Montgomery County Public Library. Used with permission.

POLICY ON UNATTENDED CHILDREN

It is the policy of the library to provide a safe and appropriate environment for library users of all ages. The library is, however, a public building with staff trained to provide public library services. The library is not equipped, nor is it the library's role, to provide long- or short-term daycare for children of any age. Aside from the planned programs, services, and activities designed for specific age groups, the library's staff is not responsible for supervising or tending to the needs of individual users or groups of users.

Accordingly, children under the age of 8 must always be accompanied by a parent, guardian, or responsible childcare provider while in the library. If a child under the age of 8 is attending a library program or activity, the parent, guardian, or responsible childcare provider must remain in the Children's Department throughout the program.

In general, parents of any minor children should not leave them unattended for long periods at the library. This is especially important in the evening. The library closes at 9 P.M. or at 5 P.M., and children should be picked up no later than five minutes before closing time. Police will be notified concerning any children left alone at the library after closing time.

Parents are responsible for the behavior of their children in the library, whether or not the parents are present.

Approved by the Board of Trustees
March 10, 1997
From West Warwick, Rhode Island, Public Library. Used with permission.

4. Customer Service Language

CUSTOMER SERVICE LANGUAGE MANUAL

1. For those whose delinquency is based on one lost book:

   "If you bring in the book, the maximum fine will be $5.00. That's better than paying $14.95 for the book."

   "We can hold these books you want to check out for a few days until you bring the book back."

   "Once your book is returned, you will only owe for the fines."

2. You owe a fine on this book. (don't say delinquent.)

   (A) Use a question to inform them.

   "Are you aware that you owe $3.75?"

   "Did you know you owe $.25?"

   (B) Other ways

   One option is to leave the word "you" out. Sometimes, doing this takes the personal issue out of the discussion, making it more matter-of-fact, not me vs. you.

   "There's a fine against this card."

   "The computer shows you have some late fees."

   When people ask about small amounts, mention that the computer keeps track of the fines.

   If the word "fines" bothers you, use "overdue charges" or "late fees" instead.

   (C) If patrons say they've paid the fine, you can waive it and say:

   "I'll clear it for you this time."

   Give cash register receipt, circle the amount and date it and say, "As of today, you have no more charges."

   (D) We can increase patrons' awareness by mentioning to them they have fines each time they check out materials.

3. That's a reference book and you can't check it out.

    Some patrons might not understand what a reference book is so you may have to explain this first:

    "We make some books reference, which means they stay in the library and are used daily by lots of people. We want to make them available for this use."

    "This is a reference book for use here in the library only. You are welcome to make copies."

    Try to find something comparable that can be checked out.

    One branch puts green dots next to the barcodes to give visual cue when charging.

    Check for circulating copies.

Samples from the manual created by the Dayton and Montgomery County Public Library. Used with permission.

5. Sample Patron Rules

PATRON RULES OF CONDUCT

Hickory Public Library's Disruptive Behavior Policy (adopted 1991)

The policy of the Hickory Public Library is to offer a full range of library service to all residents of the community, regardless of age, sex, racial or ethnic origin, religion, or economic status. The library intends to provide its services with a minimum of regulations and restriction, adopting only those which are absolutely essential to the library's operation.

The library recognizes that users of the library are in fact the owners of the library. As user-owners, the public has certain expectations. These include an outstanding collection of library materials, pleasant and attractive surroundings, and courteous, efficient and effective service from the staff.

Library users have a right to assume that visits to the library will be free from harassment, free from physical discomfort and danger, and free from psychological or emotional stress.

The library staff has essentially the same rights. Each member of the staff should be able to do his or her work free of harassment, abuse, discomfort, and undue psychological stress.

The rights of both the public and the staff are sometimes violated by the attitudes and behavior of a small number of persons.

The goal of the Library's Disruptive Behavior Policy is to minimize the effect of unacceptable behavior by defining such behavior, and authorizing library staff to take necessary steps to stop unacceptable behavior when it occurs.

Therefore, it shall be the Library's policy to maintain a quiet, pleasant environment conducive to serious study as well as casual use. To ensure the successful implementation of this policy, the following is seen as unacceptable behavior:

Loud conversation or laughter which is disturbing to other users.

Obscene or abusive language.

Smoking inside the building.

Use of radios or tape recorders so that sound is transmitted to others.

Willful destruction of or damage to any library property.

Blocking or in any way interfering with the free movement of any person or persons.

Bringing animals other than guide dogs into the library.

Removal of any library property from the building without authorization through established lending procedures.

Use of rest rooms for meetings, loitering, or consuming alcoholic beverages or using illicit drugs.

Solicitation for immoral purposes.

Soliciting or selling of any kind.

Distribution of leaflets or posting of notices not specifically authorized by the library staff.

Use of library telephone by any person other than library staff unless approved.

Consumption of food or beverages unless approved by library staff.

Following staff or others around the building, or other harassing behavior.

Rearranging or moving any library furniture or equipment from one location to another.

Sleeping.

Lovemaking.

All members of the library staff have the authority to take necessary steps when this policy is violated.

Disruptive behavior most often occurs within the library buildings, but may also occur outside on library grounds or in the parking lots. This policy covers disturbances both inside the library and on the library grounds.

Last modified 08/03/98
Sample from Hickory, North Carolina, Public Library. Used with permission.

Rules for Use of Library

The Library facility is intended to preserve books and related materials in organized collections for reading and quiet study.

The patrons of the Evanston Public Library are expected to behave in a manner that does not disturb other Library patrons, disrupt the operation of the Library, or endanger library materials.

The Library's rules are designed to promote the safety and security of the Library's patrons and collections, and to insure that the Library remains conducive to reading and study.

Library patrons are not permitted to:

1. Interfere with another person's use of the Library or with Library personnel's performance of their duties.

2. Consume food or beverages in the Library.

3. Lie or lounge on the floor, or sleep anywhere in the Library.

4. Lie down on furniture, put feet up on furniture, or move furniture other than chairs at tables.

5. Smoke anywhere in the Library.

6. Play audio equipment so that others can hear it. The use of head sets is permitted as long as such use does not disturb other Library patrons.

7. Talk loudly, make noise, use abusive or threatening language, or engage in other disruptive conduct.

8. Bring animals into the Library, except those needed to assist a patron with a disability.

9. Use the Library's rest rooms as laundry facilities, bathing facilities, or gathering places.

10. Use Library facilities, other than public lockers, to store personal belongings.

11. Leave children who are in need of supervision unattended.

12. Solicit anywhere in the Library.

13. Bring a bicycle inside the building.

14. Use roller skates, roller blades, or skateboards on Library property.

15. Go without shoes inside the building.

Any person who deliberately mutilates or removes without authorization any part of the library collection, building, or furnishings is guilty of a misdemeanor.

The police will be called when Library patrons willfully and persistently violate Library rules or engage in criminal acts. After calling the police to the Library, staff members will cooperate with law enforcement officials. The Library's staff will file criminal charges and seek criminal prosecution if law enforcement officials believe that it is appropriate.

All Library staff members are responsible for maintaining order in the Library. When staff members observe a rule being violated, they are expected to enforce the rule or to report the violation to their supervisor. When enforcing Library rules, staff members are expected to maintain a calm, non-judgmental attitude, to avoid a loud tone of voice, and to avoid the use of phrases that might be considered to be condescending.

7.1.1 Suspension of Library Privileges

The Illinois Revised Statutes, Chapter 81, Paragraph 4-7, permit the Library Board "To exclude from use of the library any person who willfully violates the rules prescribed by the board."

Library privileges may be suspended for the following reasons:

1. damaging Library property
2. stealing Library materials
3. physically harming staff or patrons
4. persistent, willful violations of the Library's posted rules of conduct.

Suspensions will be for a definite time period, not to exceed twelve months. The length of a suspension will be determined by the Library Director or other designated staff. Suspensions will apply to all Library facilities. Patrons who attempt to enter a Library facility while their Library privileges are suspended will be reported to the police for criminal trespass.

Any suspension of Library privileges longer than one day may be appealed to the Library Board. Notice of an appeal of a suspension should be made in writing to the Library Director within two weeks of receipt of the notice of suspension. The Library Director will inform the appellant of the date of the meeting at which the appeal will be heard. Any notice of appeal received later than a week before the next regularly scheduled Board meeting will be held until the following Board meeting.

From Evanston, Illinois, Public Library. Used with permission.

Conduct in Libraries Policy

In order to ensure safety and security and provide a suitable environment for library use, the following guidelines for conduct have been approved by the Library Board of Trustees:

1. All persons are welcome in the library. Parents or guardians are responsible for the conduct and safety of persons under their care.

2. The Library is not responsible for personal belongings left unattended. Personal items left by patrons who are not present on Library property are subject to disposal.

3. Library materials must be properly checked out at the circulation desk. Certain materials, such as reference books, periodicals and vertical file materials may not be removed from the library.

4. Library furniture and equipment available for public use must be used for their intended purpose.

5. Library staff reserves the right to inspect all bags, briefcases, backpacks, containers, books and any similar items.

6. Pay telephones are provided for patron use. Library telephones are for library business only. In deference to other library users, library staff will not page patrons.

7. Library materials not currently in use by patrons should be returned to staff or designated areas to be returned to their proper place. The Library staff is responsible for clearing materials not currently in use by patrons.

The following forms of conduct are not permitted.

1. Behavior which may result in disturbing other library users, including, but not limited to: loud talking, running, shoving, throwing things, physical or verbal harassment or threats.

2. Unauthorized or unscheduled group meetings or activities.

3. Food and beverages, except in approved areas by prior arrangement.

4. Use of tobacco, alcohol or illegal substances.

5. Entering the library without proper attire, which conforms to the standard of the community for public places, including shoes and shirts. Patrons whose bodily hygiene is so offensive as to constitute a nuisance to other persons shall be required to leave the building.

6. Damage, destruction, theft or improper use of library property or facilities.

7. Sleeping.

8. Carrying, displaying or drawing any unauthorized or dangerous weapon.

9. Entering non-public areas such as staff work rooms, offices and storage areas.

10. Animals, except service animals, unless authorized.

11. Any form of sexual misconduct, including exposure, offensive touching, or sexual harassment of other patrons or staff.

12. Selling, advertising, petitioning, or soliciting for contributions or support, except as authorized.

13. Any illegal act or conduct in violation of federal, state, or local law, ordinance or regulation.

Approved: DeKalb County Library Board of Trustees—December 1, 1997.

From DeKalb County (Ga.) Public Library. Used with permission.

General Customer Behavior Expectations

In order to maintain the Library's mission as a reliable community resource, in a comfortable and welcoming atmosphere for all, we ask that you observe the following expectation of customer behavior:

1. In respect of the rights of others, please maintain low noise levels. Listening devices should not be audible to anyone but yourself.

2. We welcome your use of the Library and its property, but please use it as intended, rather than as a lounging area.

3. Smoking is not allowed anywhere inside the building.

4. Please do not eat or drink inside the building or bring opened containers with you.

5. For safety and hygiene reasons, shoes must be worn by all, and customers are asked to wear appropriate street clothing.

6. Only assistive animals are permitted in the building.

7. Please do not enter staff work areas, except the Human Resources office on the fifth floor, and then only on business.

8. If you need to use a phone, please use the public telephones on the first floor.

9. Bicycling, skateboarding and roller skating on Library property are a safety hazard to our other customers. Customers are requested to carry skateboards and roller blades while in the Library or on Library property.

10. Please respect the rights of others to quietly study, read or work without interference.

11. Standards of personal hygiene are required to conform to community standards for public places. Persons whose bodily hygiene causes other customers to complain may be asked to leave.

Customers who do not respect the rights of others may be asked to leave the Library.

From Kansas City Public Library. Used with permission.

Library Rules of Conduct

It is our intention to provide library visitors with good service in a pleasant atmosphere. Each of you can help by observing the following rules of conduct.

1. Conduct that disturbs library users or staff, or that hinders others from using the library or library materials is prohibited.

2. Damage, destruction or theft of library property is prohibited. Parents are liable for all acts of minors. (Nevada Revised Statute 379.160)

3. Use of tobacco is prohibited in the library.

4. Food or beverages are prohibited in the library except for pre-approved events or in specified areas.

5. Sleeping is prohibited on library property.

6. Selling or solicitation is prohibited on library property.

7. Animals, except handicapped aide animals, are prohibited on library property.

8. Shoes and shirts must be worn in the library.

9. A child under the age of 10 years should be under the supervision of a person who assumes responsibility for him or her. Parents or adult

caregivers should monitor all activities and behavior of their children while they are in the library. If a minor—anyone under the age of 18 —is left at a library at closing time, does not follow the Library Rules of Conduct, or an emergency situation exists, then the staff person in charge will attempt to contact the parents or adult caregivers. If the parents or adult caregivers cannot be contacted, staff will immediately notify the police.

10. Library patrons may bring all items which, when placed together, fit into a box which will be placed in the foyer of each library. The interior dimensions of that box shall be 24" x 18" x 20". All items of personal property which collectively fit into this container will be allowed into the library provided such items comply with any other relevant library policy and/or law.

11. Any person creating or emanating an odor that can be detected from six feet away, will be asked to leave the library until the situation can be corrected. Before ejection of any patron who creates such a disturbance, the acting librarian shall contact by telephone appointed representatives to act in an advisory capacity. If the representative determines that the person is not making a disturbance, the patron shall not be ejected. In the event the representative does not arrive within 30 minutes, the patron can be evicted.

Adopted by the Las Vegas–Clark County Library District Board of Trustees on February 12, 1991.

Revised and adopted December 10, 1991, October 10, 1996, and October 9, 1997.

From the Las Vegas–Clark County (Nev.) Library. Used with permission.

Rights of Library Users

The Omaha Public Library believes all customers have the right to use library services and materials without being disturbed by other library users. All customers and staff have the right to a safe and comfortable environment, as well as facilities and materials which are in good condition.

1. Treat library customers and staff with courtesy and respect.

    Do not interrupt or disturb the work of other customers.

    Do not annoy or harass another person.

Do not use abusive or obscene language.

Do not disturb dog guides or hearing aid dogs; pets are not allowed.

You must wear shoes and a shirt while in the library.

2. Treat library materials and property with respect.

Do not mutilate books or other library materials—use photocopiers and leave information intact for other customers.

Check out any library materials being taken out of the building.

Do not deface or damage library property.

Keep your feet off the furniture.

3. Eating, drinking or use of tobacco products is not allowed in the library.

4. Do not bring alcoholic beverages into library; intoxication is prohibited.

5. No soliciting or panhandling is allowed.

6. Do not sleep or utilize the library as a hotel.

Failure to follow these rules of conduct will result in the person being asked to leave the library. Violators who refuse to leave the library will be arrested and prosecuted for criminal trespass.

Please notify a security guard or a librarian if someone is disrupting your right to use the library. We also ask that you not leave your possessions or children unattended, especially children under the age of six.

From the Omaha Public Library. Used with permission.

Rules of Conduct Policy

In order to provide an environment in which all customers may safely and freely use and enjoy the library, some expectations regarding behavior must be enforced. Anyone observing proper conduct in the library is allowed to freely make use of the library. Those whose behavior is disruptive to library operations and/or to others in the library may have the privilege of using the library abridged or denied to the extent necessary to deal with the problem.

Library staff make every effort to apply these rules in as fair, humane, and positive manner as possible. All staff members have the right to deny access to the Library if, in their judgment, these rules have been abused.

Library staff may contact the Lafayette Police for assistance if deemed advisable.

Library users shall be engaged in activities associated with the use of a public library while in the building. The following list includes examples of activities that are prohibited, and which may lead to denial of library privileges:

Damaging, abusing, or vandalizing library property

Smoking

Eating or drinking, except in designated areas

Bringing animals into the library other than assistive animals

Possession of a weapon unless in performance of official duties

Behavior that may be reasonably expected to result in injury to self or others

Engaging in any illegal activity

Users shall respect the rights of other users and staff and shall not harass or annoy others by:

Noisy or boisterous behavior including talking, singing, or playing music loudly enough to disturb others

Physical, verbal, visual, or sexual harassment or threats to other users or staff

Behavior that may be reasonably expected to disturb other users or staff

Unauthorized soliciting of funds or offering goods or services for sale in a public area

Body odor so offensive as to present a nuisance to others

Persons whose actions violate these rules may be asked to stop such actions. The Library reserves the right to require anyone violating these rules of conduct to leave the Library. The Library may withdraw permission for a person to re-enter the building if the person continues violating the rules.

From Lafayette, Colorado, Public Library. Used with permission.

6. Sample from the Ontario (Calif.) Public Library Procedure Manual

DISRUPTIVE BEHAVIOR: PHYSICAL VIOLENCE

Persons who engage in fighting may be guilty of assault, battery, and disturbing the peace and may be liable for property damage. (California Penal Code Sec. 240, 242, 245, 415)

Staff Procedure—Adults Fighting

1. Call the police at 9-911 immediately.
2. Call other staff members to witness and to assist in calmly directing other customers away from the area.
3. Depending on the situation, attempt to stop the fighting from a distance. Do not try to get in between the persons fighting.
4. Take notes and be prepared to describe the account to the Police. Ask victims and witnesses to stay until the police arrive.
5. Fill out a Customer Incident form.

Staff Procedure—Children Fighting

1. Attempt to stop the fight. Clearly tell the children to stop and sit down away from each other.
2. Direct other customers away from the area, including friends of fighters.
3. Assess injuries.
4. Talk to fighters about the problem. Attempt to resolve the issue.
5. Warn older children and teens that the Police will be called if fighting starts again.

DISRUPTIVE BEHAVIOR: SLEEPING

Sleeping is not a problem unless it is disturbing other customers (e.g., person sprawled out on furniture or floor, taking too much room, or being noisy).

Sleeping may also be considered "Loitering." (California Penal Code Sec. 647e)

Staff Procedure

1. If the sleeper is disturbing other customers, approach him/her from the front, remaining at arm's length. Do not touch the sleeping customer. Example: Rap the table or wall to awaken the customer.

2. Speak quietly, identifying yourself as a staff member. Inform the customer that s/he is causing a disturbance for other customers by sleeping in the library. Warn that s/he will be asked to leave the library if the prohibited behavior continues.

3. If the prohibited behavior continues, obtain staff support and jointly ask the customer to leave the library.

4. If the customer refuses, call Police at 9-911.

5. If the situation warrants, fill out a Customer Incident form.

DISRUPTIVE BEHAVIOR: STRANDED MINORS

A child with no means of getting home at closing is a stranded minor. Library policy requires two staff members to wait with a minor child to avoid potential liability. (California Penal Code Sec. 270, 271)

Staff Procedure

1. Five minutes before closing, staff should determine whether children under 16 have a means of getting home.

2. When locking the front door, Adult Services staff should check to see if any minors are waiting outside.

3. If the child has no means of getting home, try to phone the parents.

4. If the child still has not been picked up at closing, two staff members must wait with the child. Do not transport the child.

5. Fifteen minutes after the library closes to the public, staff should contact the Police and ask that the Department assume responsibility for the child.

6. If the situation warrants, fill out a Customer Incident form.

DISRUPTIVE BEHAVIOR: TALKING/SOCIALIZING

Excessive noise in the library is disturbing to other customers. Staff should be aware of noisy and overbearing talkers. Other users may be too intimidated to complain, and they are often reluctant to move elsewhere because library study space is not always easily found.

In case of disruptive children, refer to the section on "Disruptive Children." (California Ed. Code Sec. 18960)

Staff Procedure

1. Approach noisy users and politely ask that they keep their voices down because others are trying to study.

2. If the noise continues to be unbearable, approach noisy users and tell them they will be asked to leave the library if the noise continues.

3. If noise continues, obtain staff support and approach the noisy users. Ask them to leave the library.

4. If they refuse, call Police at 9-911.

5. Fill out a Customer Incident form if customer refuses to leave or Police are called.

DISRUPTIVE BEHAVIOR: VERBAL ALTERCATIONS BETWEEN CUSTOMERS

(Violation of California Penal Code Sec. 415)

Staff Procedures

1. Move other customers away from the area in a calm and firm manner.

2. Attempt to defuse the situation before it becomes physically abusive. Do not put yourself, other customers, or other staff in danger.

3. If the situation appears threatening, call the Police at 9-911.
4. Identify the customers involved. Take note of physical descriptions. Be prepared to give detailed information to the Police Officer responding.
5. Fill out a Customer Incident form.

ABERRANT BEHAVIOR: GENERAL

Behavior defined as aberrant in this section is usually caused by psychological problems or substance abuse. Examples are talking to oneself, pacing the aisles, staring, unsteady walking and overly loud talking.

Please be aware that some medical conditions, e.g., diabetes, may cause symptoms similar to those normally associated with intoxication.

Staff Procedure

1. If the aberrant behavior is not disturbing other customers or staff, it should be tolerated.
2. Do not touch the customer, but visually check for a medical alert tag around wrist or neck. If the customer is able to function and does not need assistance, treat him/her as you would any other customer.
3. If the customer appears to be ill or to need personal assistance, ask if you can be of help. Offer to call either the Paramedics at 9-911 or a family member if it is not an emergency.
4. If the person becomes disruptive, follow the procedures outlined in the section on "Disruptive Behavior," incorporating the special guidelines given on the following pages for dealing with:
    a) emotionally disturbed persons
    b) lonely/possessive helpless persons
    c) persons suspected of being under the influence of alcohol or drugs.
5. If the situation warrants, fill out a Customer Incident form.

ABERRANT BEHAVIOR: PERSONS SUSPECTED OF BEING UNDER THE INFLUENCE OF ALCOHOL OR DRUGS

Persons under the influence of alcohol can generally be detected by their alcoholic breath, but it is often difficult to determine the presence of drugs when a person is behaving in an aberrant manner. Such behavior may also be caused by physiological disorders. In either case, exercise caution in approaching such persons, since the person may exhibit sudden and extreme mood changes. (California Penal Code Sec. 647f)

Staff Procedure

1. Get another staff member to serve as back-up support. Have a pre-arranged signal for calling the Police.

2. Remember to look for a medical alert tag.

3. Do not make the person feel watched or cornered. Stay at a safe distance. Do not touch the person.

4. If you need to assist the person with locating library materials, do not go alone with him/her to remote areas of library.

5. If the person cannot function normally, ask the person calmly, "Are you ill? Do you need medical assistance?" Call paramedics at 9-911 if needed.

6. At the first sign of dangerous behavior, call or have a colleague call 9-911.

7. If the customer is disruptive, ask him/her to stop. Give warning that if the behavior continues, s/he will be asked to leave the library.

8. If the customer persists, obtain the support of other staff and ask customer to leave the library.

9. If the customer refuses to leave, call Police at 9-911.

10. If the situation warrants, fill out a Customer Incident form.

CRIMINAL BEHAVIOR: CHILD ABUSE

Abuse is "a situation where any person willfully causes or permits any child to suffer, or inflict thereon, unjustifiable physical pain or mental suffering, or having the care or custody of any child, willfully causes or permits the person or health of the child to be placed in a situation such that his or her person or health is endangered." (Crime Abuse Prevention Handbook; Office of the Attorney General.)

Examples: excessive physical punishment, including hitting with a closed fist, kicking or twisting arms, or leaving a child in a closed car in the summer sun. (California Penal Code Sec. 1164, 11165.2, 11165.3, 11165.4, 11165.6)

Staff Procedure

1. If the child's life is in danger, or abuse is severe, call the Police at 9-911.

2. If the child is in less immediate danger or has left the library, try to obtain the name and address of the child if possible. Customer records may be used for this purpose.

3. Report the name and address and a description of the incident to the Child Abuse Hotline 9-945-3777. You need not investigate the incident or provide witnesses to make a report.

Note: Hotline reports are confidential. The Department of Public Social Services will investigate the report. If possible, the victim will be interviewed at school.

Used with permission.

Bibliography

Adamec, Christine A. *How to Live with a Mentally Ill Person: A Handbook of Day-to-Day Strategies*. New York: Wiley, 1996.

The Columbia University College of Physicians and Surgeons Complete Home Guide to Mental Health. Ed. Frederic I. Kass, John M. Oldham, and Herbert Pardes. New York: Holt, 1995.

Korpell, Herbert S. *How You Can Help: A Guide for Families of Psychiatric Hospital Patients*. Washington, D.C.: American Psychiatric Pr., 1984.

Nichols, Michael P. *The Lost Art of Listening*. New York: Guilford, 1995.

Woolis, Rebecca. *When Someone You Love Has a Mental Illness: A Handbook for Family, Friends, and Caregivers*. Los Angeles: Tarcher, 1992.

For additional information on mental illness and programs, materials, legislation, etc., concerning mental illness, see the Web site of the National Mental Health Association at http://www.nmha.org

Index

MARK WILLIS is Community Relations Manager in the Dayton and Montgomery County Public Library. He presents talks on this topic through ALA and other organizations